Dancing
with the
Stars

NORMAN BORINE

ISBN: 978-1-60414-022-4 / 1-60414-022-4

Fideli – rev. 12/2007

Also by Norman Borine:

King Dragon - The Unauthorized Biobraphy of Bruce Lee

www.bruceleekingdragon.com

Hollywood
Once upon a time

A story of MGM in the Forties,

a time never to come again.

Norman Borine, left, with his nephew, Bill Borine.

Bill Borine, as a tribute to his late uncle, Norman, presents *Dancing with the Stars*. Though Norman was not able to publish this work before his death, Bill has published it posthumously to show the world his uncle's amazing life. Bill remembers his uncle fondly, and hopes you will enjoy reading about his life and the stars he worked with. Visit www.dancingwiththestars.com to learn even more.

Contents

Norman Borine

Norman (above right) and Judy Garland in their first film together, "Till The Clouds Roll By." This scene included 27 of the male contract dancers at MGM in the '40s. The film's subject was the life story of composer Jerome Kern, who visited the set during shooting. 1947

Fade In

Norman Borine reveals in intimate detail the exciting and fascinating story of how he moved from a small town in Idaho to Hollywood, where he soon became a member of the elite MGM family. He explains how he went from a $100 per week "contract dancer" to become the first dance partner of Cyd Charisse, earning $1,000 per week (a remarkable salary for a dancer in the early '40s) ... and to become a "dance-in" for Fred Astaire.

Norman relates tales of dancing with Judy Garland, Gene Kelly, Ray Bolger, Lucille Ball, Lucille Bremer, Betty Hutton, Marilyn Monroe, Carmen Miranda, Vera Ellen, Eleanor Powell, Mitzi Gaynor, Yvonne De Carlo, and of swimming until waterlogged with Esther Williams. He tells amusing incidents about Marjorie Main, as well as a dramatic and humorous story about Lassie. He relates encounters on the MGM lot with Katharine Hepburn, as well as famous directors and choreographers. During times when he was loaned-out to every other major studio, his experiences were broadened ... so the list of movie greats with whom he worked goes on and on. Many of the things he relates are tales never before told.

MGM in the '40s.

CHAPTER 1

My Own Yellow Brick Road

As a child, I did a lot of dreaming. Not just at night after falling asleep, but the kind we all do throughout each day ... the "billions and billions," as Carl Sagan would say, "of both little and big (sometimes nebulous) thoughts and ideas weaving constantly in and out of our minds, regardless of where we happen to be or what we are doing during waking hours." It's interesting how this dream process goes through a series of changes as we move in and out of daily experiences and into answers.

Things were different in the '40s than they are today ... much different. Not just in Hollywood, but everywhere. Perhaps my biggest regret at this particular moment is that I didn't begin keeping a journal the day I stepped off the big red streetcar at Venice and Overland Boulevard after paying my 10 cent fare in Hollywood approximately 45 minutes earlier. The walk of a long block (or was it two, I can't be quite certain) seemed more like a mile, as I reverted to my childhood dreams. What would it actually be like? How would I act? What would I say? More than ever, I suddenly realized something: Dreams really do come true. Since the age of eight I had dreamed of working in the movies.

The colossal building coming closer with every step was proof that my dream was about to become a reality.

Today is the day I will sign a seven-year movie contract with the world's largest and most prestigious studio, home to more movie stars than any other studio. These thoughts raced back and forth across my mind, over and over again. As I approached Washington Boulevard, I didn't simply walk across when the signal turned green. It was more like I floated to the other side. I glanced at the Greek columns and wrought iron gate. There was a sign with a large red arrow pointing left and lettering that informed me I should walk left, turn right, and use the auto gate.

I stopped dead in my tracks and looked at the sign again, but the information was the same. I couldn't believe it was correct. The auto gate was only for the stars and directors, people who came to the studio in chauffeur-driven limousines. Anyone would know that. I'd seen it a thousand times in the movie magazines I'd read. I continued to walk, stare like a tourist and quiver with anticipation. After turning right, my gaze was directed upward, stopping on what had been indelibly stamped upon my 26-year-old mind since age eight. There they were, the giant iron letters shouting to all the world that this was, indeed, the world of METRO GOLDWYN MAYER. For all like myself who had difficulty believing it, there was Leo the Lion, mouth open wide, roaring: ARS GRATIA ARTIS.

Approaching the window at the left of the gate, my questioning words to the guard were lost as he got up from his chair and stepped through the door facing the studio. Over my shoulder, I heard him say courteously, "Good morning, Miss Dietrich. It's a pleasure to see you again." He gave a slight bow, and then nodded to the chauffeur as the long black limo passed slowly through the gate, apparently unconcerned by Leo sitting high above the gate.

I don't know how long I stood gaping at the disappearing star in her limo. The next thing I was aware of was the guard asking (no doubt for the second or third time) what I wanted; did I have a pass? No, I told him, I didn't have a pass ... I was here to see Mr. Cordner in casting. He did his nodding thing again and returned to the booth. He picked up the phone, and in a matter of seconds leaned up to the hole in the window and motioned me toward the last building on the right. I wasted no time floating through the magic gate, turned right, and continued on to the last building. What happened during the next ten or fifteen minutes remains, now more than 60 years later, somewhat shrouded in a sort of mystical fog. The bottom line was that I signed on the dotted line and, moment by moment, became aware that this place was to become my home, so to speak, for the next seven years.

"Your first assignment will be working with Judy Garland in *Till the Clouds Roll By*. There's no actual starting date yet, but you're guaranteed 48 weeks' pay for each of the seven years, even during days or weeks when there may be no actual work. You'll possibly be loaned out to other major studios from time to time ... at the same rate, of course. Meanwhile, you are to be on call at all times. When you're not home, be sure someone is there who knows how to reach you." The secretary told me as she handed me a copy of the contract. "Feel free to call me any time if you have questions, Norman. I'm sure you're going to be very happy here." As she finished the sentence, the phone rang and I headed out through the door and into the beginning of my dreams.

I signed the contract and left the casting office as though on my own "Yellow Brick Road." After all, the secretary had said, "Your first assignment will be with Judy Garland." No wonder my feet barely touched the ground as I retraced my steps. I nodded a thank-you to the polite guard who had pointed me toward "the last building on the right" only a few moments ago. Pretending to already feel comfortable and at home, I stole a backward glance at Leo the Lion, just to assure myself that what

All of us together with Judy for the first time in "Till The Clouds Roll By." Norman is the first man on the left.

I'd done had not been just another dream. Reassured that he and everything else I'd just encountered was real, I walked back around the building, crossed the street on the green light and headed back to Venice Boulevard. Soon aboard the next streetcar, feeling like it was my own private gondola, I floated once more through Beverly Hills and back to Hollywood.

Remember, this was 1943. All at once, I became aware that I would be assured of an income. I could pay the rent on the small house where I'd lived since 1941. It set me back $20 a month, plus phone and utilities. Considering I'd been somehow managing on $8 a week and an average of less than a dollar in tips, I felt like the floodgates of heaven had opened. Recalling the words of the secretary: "... and whether you work or not, you'll receive a paycheck beginning next Friday, with a guarantee of 48 weeks each year for the next seven."

The voice of the conductor broke into my reverie: "Santa Monica and Vine ... next stop ... Santa Monica and Vine." My hand automatically reached up and pulled the cord. The spell was broken and I was no longer floating in my gondola somewhere in the clouds above the rainbow. Excited and aware of the beginning of a totally new adventure, I stepped down from the red car and heard its doors woosh closed behind me.

The sign near the drive-in at the corner reminded me I was back in Hollywood, and for a moment there was a feeling of disappointment. Heading toward the building, I recalled all I'd experienced only an hour before regained my joy. It was as if Judy and I were skipping between the cars, traveling along the Yellow Brick Road and through the doors of the drive-in together. Never had the coffee tasted so good, and for the first time I didn't begrudge the 10 cents it cost me. After all, I was a rich man! I'd be able to quit my job at the parking lot this weekend; I'd give notice tonight and hope Tarzan (Johnny Weissmuller) would return at least once more before my final night. If he drank enough at the bar

Judy Garland was one of
Norman's favorite movie stars.

where he sometimes hung out, he might ask me to drive him home again. In that case, his usual 25 cent tip could possibly become $2 ... the biggest I'd ever gotten. Then I could stop at the Hollywood Ranch Market on the way home and load up on groceries, plus a 25-pound hunk of ice from the ice machine outside. Even if Johnny didn't show up, the ice was only a nickel and I could always count on that much in tips, even during a slow evening.

As thoughts went through my head, Judy somehow slipped out the door when I paid for the coffee. I walked outside, but she was nowhere in sight. Walking slowly along my own Yellow Brick Road to 1018 N. Vine, just a short block and a half away, I opened the door of the little house I'd already learned to love, and wasn't surprised to hear, off in the distance of my mind, a familiar voice saying, "There's no place like home ... no place like home."

When the phone rang one afternoon three weeks and three paychecks (without working) later, it was not the voice of Judy, but the news it brought was so great I could scarcely refrain from yelling at the top of my voice. Yes, it was Jeanette, the secretary in casting, politely informing me I should, "... please report to Rehearsal Hall A at 9 o'clock tomorrow morning, with rehearsal clothes. You will be working for Bob Alton. The picture is *Till the Clouds Roll By*, with Judy Garland." That was it. For a split second I couldn't move. Dead silence ... then, like the roar of a lion, I let out a yell and collapsed on the floor in absolute ecstasy ... knowing that at long last my new life was truly about to begin.

The ride the next morning on the big red car was strangely similar to the one nearly a month before, but the walk from Venice Boulevard was most definitely different. The moment I stepped down from the car, my mind transformed the sidewalk and pavement into yellow bricks bordered with multi-colored flowers, and there were Munchkins skipping along with me, singing: "Follow the Yellow

Robert Alton's MGM test shots.

Brick Road." The road led me straight to *the* gate. The same guard was seated inside, and he greeted me politely by name and gave me directions to the rehearsal hall.

I turned, winked at Leo in his guardian position above the gate, and walked past the casting office, where I received a hearty greeting of, "Hi, young fella, beautiful morning!" He was gone before I was aware he'd been speaking to me. The voice was unmistakable — it was Jimmy Durante! It wasn't Clark Gable or Robert Taylor, but a warm glow came over me, assuring me this was truly going to be home, not just a place to work.

Suddenly I looked up, my heart skipped a beat and I did a double take. There, against a framed gold background, were letters spelling out: REHEARSAL HALL A. I stood transfixed for a moment before entering the huge sliding door that was partially open. I was about to meet my new family; all of the young dancers with whom I would soon be working with for the next seven whole years in more than sixty films.

I soon learned that most of the dancers had been brought to Hollywood (MGM, Culver City, to be exact), from New York by Robert Alton, who recently had been lured from Broadway where he had a total of five musicals running. When he first arrived, so he informed me later, he'd been disappointed at the lack of quality and number of dancers available, hence his decision to import a large number who had worked for him in the Big Apple. Because of the salary and the heretofore nonexistent possibility of a seven-year contract, these young people had served notice and left the super-big musicals where they'd been working. They, too, were aware that this was the golden era of musicals, never-to-come-again. It was an honor just being a part of it all. Being asked to work for the world's largest and most prestigious studio, and being paid large salaries were just icing on the cake. Yes, we were the lucky ones, the chosen few — and we knew it.

A very young Judy Garland walking down the street and sitting atop a piano (Chicago, 1934).

To those not familiar with big names working creatively behind the scenes and cameras, it may mean little or nothing when I say I was excited to find Roger Edens as our rehearsal pianist, and Kay Thompson as our vocal coach. (Ten years later, Kay was primarily identified with Andy Williams and his brothers, and headlined as Kay Thompson and the Williams Brothers. They were tremendously popular at the time.) Kay could play a wild piano and belt out a song like no one else. Kay was Judy Garland's vocal coach. Anticipating involvement with both of them was even more cause for me to be nervous.

The first morning passed so quickly I was truly disappointed when Bob, Kay, and Roger disappeared and the assistant called out, "Okay, everybody, lunch, one hour. Be back at one." A few minutes later, seated outside the hall eating a sack lunch with most of the other dancers who preferred to bask in the sun rather than spend time and money in the studio commissary. My spirits took a major spiral upward when suddenly, from out of nowhere, a small pick-up truck pulled up beside us. A man got out, walked around

Judy Garland as she appeared in "Till the Clouds Roll By." She remained Norman's favorite actress-dancer throughout his seven years at MGM.

the truck and removed a director's chair. As he disappeared into the rehearsal hall, I could plainly read the four magic letters in bold print across the back: JUDY.

Lunch now became a feast as my mind conjured up all sorts of images including Kansas, Auntie Em, the Yellow Brick Road, The Wizard, the Ruby Slippers, and Toto. Before I realized it, the hands of the clock pointed to one o'clock. In a few minutes, we were perspiring as we worked on an intricate combination with the assistant choreographer. Suddenly everything stopped ... at least in my mind, though physically all of us continued to dance. Out of the corner of my eye, with no fanfare, I saw Judy walk through the door with Bob, Kay, and Roger. She had a wonderful smile and her gaze drifted toward us as she made her way to the piano. Somehow it had truly never occurred to me how tiny she was, but then I'd only seen her on the silver screen until now.

Bob immediately called for us to take a break. Instead of heading outside to bask in the sun, we casually hung around, watching and listening as Judy stood next to Roger, who began working out an introduction to the number we had already begun, "Who stole my heart away, who makes me dream all day." While Kay sorted through sheets of music scattered across the huge concert grand, Bob was the only one making use of his director's chair. The others leaned casually against the piano, obviously intrigued by Roger's arrangement of the song. Seeing the names in heavy black lettering on those chairs brought out a determination in me to see my own name spelled out on canvas one day. Right now, it was still a part of the dream ... a part which would happen in less than a year.

Unlike the mad rush and pace of today's movie studio routine, the rest of that first afternoon in the rehearsal hall (though I was unaware of it at the time) was typical of what all of us would experience during most of the seven years to follow ... a laid-back atmosphere. Work, of course, was serious. The powers that be had not combed Hollywood and New York City for the best dancers they could find to complement the top Stars without demanding quality results. Yet the pace was relaxed and friendly, an integral part of what was then termed the MGM Family.

Regardless of the amount of work to be done, there was always time to get more done. If something planned for one day was not complete, it was continued on the following day, with no attempt to make up for lost time. If the budget for a particular film was six months, it was not uncommon that it be extended to nine. If it was a year, it might well go on for eighteen months or even two years. If there was stress or pandemonium anywhere, it was not visible to the performers. Even the producers, who often came to the set during a rehearsal to sit in a director's chair and watch some dramatic scene being shot with Hepburn, Gable, Astaire or Turner, were calm.

Yes, things were casual, regardless of technical involvement, primarily because there was plenty of time and, more importantly, plenty of money. There was absolutely no practice or concern for dollars spent superseding quality when it came to producing entertainment ... whether comedy, drama, or the musical.

Seeing Judy Garland on this first day was the beginning of what it was like to participate in creating a finished product, which was in most cases, both exciting and satisfying. It was the opening of a door to lifelong memories of caring and sharing with others who enjoyed not only the work and success, but also the everyday camaraderie. Perhaps in the long run, this was the greatest reward.

Sometime during the afternoon following proper and friendly introductions, all of us gathered around the piano (or as close as we could, due to mere numbers) and listened to Roger, Kay, and Judy. As we swayed to the music, they hummed and memorized the lyrics. Then everything stopped, just as it had when Judy had arrived. A propman hurriedly slid two unmarked director's chairs close to the others and the huge doorway slid aside to admit Arthur Freed, our producer. We'd been told he would be visiting at some point during the afternoon. With him, much to everyone's surprise, was a very special guest...the one and only Jerome Kern, composer of the music we were working on. Each of us felt the honor and privilege of meeting one of the truly great composers of the time.

The remainder of the day was taken up with an extended coffee break, followed by a run-through of the number we'd rehearsed with Bob and his assistant earlier in the day. When our guests departed, we joined forces to polish what we had thus far accomplished, before being casually dismissed and given our call for next morning. With a "thanks for the good work, kids" from our choreographer, plus a friendly acknowledgment from Judy, Kay, and Roger, we were done for the day.

In retrospect, to say that the first day of rehearsal in my new "home" was momentous is admittedly an understatement. There, in the giant hall, were not only an important pianist and vocal coach, but also three major stars from three different creative areas. Judy Garland, top MGM star, Jerome Kern, star composer of Broadway and Hollywood; and Vincente Minnelli, star MGM director (as well as husband of Judy, and soon-to-be father of Liza Minnelli), who had arrived midway through the coffee break.

To a new kid on the block (me), all of this was unbelievably impressive, to say the least, and I was silently saying a big thank-you to the universe for an experience I knew would, in numerous variations, be repeated over and over during the coming years. My contract, still more dream than reality, again loomed bigger, brighter, and more meaningful in my mind than ever.

That evening, sitting on the patio of my little Hollywood home, looking up at the stars, I was quietly aware of another meaning of stars ... one much closer, more possible to reach out and touch ... even with a possibility of becoming one. Or was this, as the song says, the impossible dream? If so, at least I could go on dancing with the stars ... them in their heaven, and I in mine. Even in that possibility I found no conflict.

Judy Garland and possibly makeup artist Del Armstrong. Armsrtong worked as an uncredited assistant makeup artist on "The Wizard of Oz" and as makeup artist for "A Star is Born" in 1948.

CHAPTER TWO

Judy, Vincente & Liza

Days passed. Weeks passed. Always it was the same. Always it was different. We were never to see Jerome Kern again ... a few weeks later he was dead, and though we didn't truly know him, we were saddened when the news came. At the same time, all of us were happy he'd visited us in person.

Dancers working in a musical film today would find it difficult to believe the amount of time spent on a production number such as the one we were working on in my first experience with Judy. With modern sophisticated cameras, particularly the zoom lens and their ease of working, the same routines can be shot in less than a week, as opposed to the three to four weeks it took us.

Most of the difference, of course, is due to our having had only a single camera, as opposed to the simultaneous use of two or more. In those days, a tremendous amount of time was spent in breaking-down and setting-up for the next shot. Depending on how involved it was, time between shots easily ran from one to three hours. Much of this time was spent adjusting the huge lights hanging from long catwalks overhead. These were suspended from the ceiling by heavy metal bars and chains, and were reached by straight up and down ladders, climbed many times daily by each of the electricians who manned the giant complicated arc lights.

Without exaggeration, we were lucky to complete two shots in an entire day when working on a production number. In order to begin shooting any new sequence, it was customary to spend an entire morning preparing a setup. Following lunch, another hour could be spent in a run through of movements to be shot and possible last minute adjustments to be made by both camera crew and electricians prior to making the first shot. I would later learn that while working with Judy there were far fewer retakes than with most stars.

Yes, the Judy with whom we became more and more acquainted was exceptional in many ways. Often to all of us, she seemed quite amazing. Though not actually a highly trained dancer in the way we were, she most definitely possessed a very special gift which gave her a natural confidence and knowledge that most of us admittedly did not have. Much of this, of course, was due to her many years performing on both stage and screen.

During nearly all rehearsals, she gave us the impression (until we knew her better) that she was scarcely interested and couldn't care less about technique, emotion or flair. To an observer seeing her for the first time and not knowing who she was, they might well wonder what she was doing and how anyone might consider her a star. Most of the time she simply walked through her part ... another trait we were to better understand after knocking ourselves out for the choreographer or director prior to their knowing our personal and individual capabilities. Judy walked, rather than danced, through

Judy Garland

many rehearsals, obviously because she knew her part and was conserving her energy for the big moments. She knew she had nothing to prove, so she would mark the steps and move along with us, and making sure she was in the right place at the right time.

When the director finally called out: "Roll 'em," the difference in her body movements and entire personality were like night and day. In fact, it wasn't long before all of us working with her nicknamed her "one-take Garland," since many were the times that having called "Cut," the director would speak briefly with the cameraman after the very first shot, then add: "OK, print it!"

Those not familiar with what goes into creating a movie (in this instance, a giant musical dance number), may fail to grasp the rarity of Judy's talent. Most generally if a second, or very rarely a third, take was required, it almost always turned out it was due to some camera or lighting goof-up rather than something Judy had either done or not done.

In working before the camera, as opposed to performing before a live audience, one of the prime rules is to be so aware of the camera that the viewer believes the character is unaware of it. In this regard, Judy was an expert. Regardless of what was going on, whether alone or with a group, long shot or close-up, she appeared very unaware that a camera was recording her every move. When chalk marks or tape were put here and there on the floor to cue the performer or the camera movement, her performance was as though the marks did not exist. She seemed to have a sixth sense that kept her from moving out of those marked boundaries. All of this, naturally, is what truly makes a star.

Many of us at this time weren't aware that the future Liza Minnelli lay quietly beneath Judy's loosely clothed exterior. Following weeks of rehearsal when shooting began; Liza began to appear more noticeably due to the form-fitting yellow gown Judy was wearing. Judy's wardrobe, with ostrich plumes below the waist, as well as sprinkles of gold sequins, failed to take attention away from Liza, who had now begun to make us aware of her approaching arrival. Those viewing the rushes from the first day of shooting noticed this. The next morning, costume designer Helen Rose arrived on the scene and wrapped Judy's waist with a soft gold lame sash ... voila no more baby bump! The rest of the number was finished without interruption. I recall one of the girls remarking that it was too bad Mr. Kern couldn't have remained with us long enough to see the entire number. He would surely have been as pleased with the routine as all of us were in dancing to the music he had composed.

A few months later during a rehearsal with Lucille Ball, we were pleasantly surprised when the door was pushed aside to admit a very, very special trio ... Judy, baby Liza, and proud father, Vincente Minnelli. Judy was carrying Liza in her arms and Vincente was watching over the two of them with a proud expression on his face. Now, with the addition of Liza, we were overwhelmed by the combination of not two, not four, but six huge eyes (three pair, if you must) smiling and blinking happily and contagiously around the hall as everyone gathered to admire the happy family.

Lucille let out a shriek of ecstasy that could be heard through the walls and onto the nearest sound stage. She immediately called the commissary, asking the caterers to rush a supply of coffee and doughnuts, plus an assortment of fruit in for the guests. Taking further command, she shouted orders at us to "take a break ... and let Judy, Vincente, and Liza know how delighted we are to have them as our guests on their very first visit to the Studio together." As if all this wasn't sufficient to prove our joy at seeing them, she led us in a cheer, counting enthusiastically, "One, two, three, hurrah! ... Oh, come on, folks, you can do better than that," to which we repeated the last exuberant word three more times. It seemed we'd barely finished our last hurrah when the door opened and the caterers arrived with not only doughnuts, coffee and fresh fruit, but an assortment of finger-sandwiches, pickles, chips with dip, and olives. The celebration was now complete and we spent the balance of the morning aware only of how special this occasion was.

Lunch time arrived all too quickly, and our visitors waved farewell as they headed off toward what we knew would be another much deserved welcome. Most of us, now more desirous of sunshine and a tan than food, headed outside with towels and chairs to enjoy the luxury of our daily sunbath. Lucille and Donahue, our new choreographer were whisked away to the commissary, while a few of our members strolled off in the same direction, leaving the rest of us to do our own thing. The dressing rooms, lockers, and restrooms were downstairs ... we had all the comforts of home.

CHAPTER THREE

Lucille, the Zany Ball

To think, say, or jot down the fact that working with Lucille Ball in "Easy to Wed," after spending weeks and weeks with Judy Garland was comparable to the difference between night and day is perhaps the understatement of the ages. Before this episode is over and the tale unfolds, even Lucille's staunchest fans may be forced to agree, though there will be those who mutter beneath their breath: "So what else is new? That's our Lucy. That's why we love her." And I agree ... so what?

The antics which cause Lucille (we never called her Lucy) to be so loved by her fans were evident from the moment she first walked through the door of Rehearsal Hall B. The sound of her raucous voice matched the remark: "Hey! What's with us having to squish and squeeze ourselves into this itty-bitty tiny little box of a room built for mice? Aren't we good enough for the big one?" She referred, of course, to Rehearsal Hall A, just the other side of the solid wall, where we'd first spent our time with

Judy. "With the salary I'm not getting," she went on, "I should think the least they could do is give me some space to work in."

Jack Donahue, who looked as much like a choreographer as Orson Welles and was about the same size, walked toward her, enfolded her in his arms, squeezed her, then let her go with an added pat on her butt, at the same time questioning: "What's all the big fuss, Honey Baby? You've got four good-looking guys here, warmed up and ready to go. Besides, you've got me, so what more could anyone want ... huh?" Donahue's tone was as flip as Lucille's had been.

"Well," drawled his opponent, "it still seems to me you would have or could have worked a little harder and pulled a few strings so we could've used the hall marked with an A instead of a B, you louse. Oh ... excuse me, I forgot you're coming up in the world and I should address you as Mr. Louse." She bowed politely placing her index finger to her pursed and pouty cupid-bow lips, at the same time batting her eyelashes, as she curtsied.

We soon learned that people in high places were quick to smile and simply wait until Lucille decided, sooner or later, to simmer down and become serious. Donahue was no exception. He fussed and fumed ... and waited for the changes.

"Well, come on, Mr. Dance Director," Lucille was now saying. "Why don't you direct us and let us get on with it? What's holding us up? What are we-all supposed to do, huh? Huh? Huh?" Each repetition was accented more strongly than the one before. Then she gave him one of her famous wide-eyed frozen stares, which was part of her stock-in-trade, causing her to be one of the funniest, zaniest, most hilarious ladies, not only at MGM, but also later at RKO, which she finally purchased and turned into her own Desilu.

The author (whose left elbow seems glued to Lucille Ball's right shoulder) stares at her through his monicle. Van Johnson and Esther Williams also starred in "Easy to Wed."—

It was times like these when we became aware of just how different the working styles of creative and talented individuals are. Judy was sublime and almost perfect. Yet here was a star who ran the gamut ... beautiful, crazy, loud and brassy, with the ability to become soft and tender. Along with all of this was an underlying intelligence, which all too often was not evident in top entertainers.

Rehearsals progressed and weeks passed. As with Judy, we dancers worked harder when it was time, then relaxed in the sun during coffee breaks and the lunch hour. Most of these timeout breaks were our usual allotted rest periods; but some occurred when discussions were going on between Lucille and Donahue, or perhaps as the two had conversations with pianist Roger Edens. Piano music was generally used until the routine was complete, after which a recording was made by the MGM Orchestra and used for final rehearsals, as well as while shooting the number.

Sometimes we'd participate, helping both the choreographer and orchestra conductor set the pace and tempo, adding certain dramatic flare, which helped the musicians see what took place as they played. In retrospect, I realize the gift we were given in being a part of entertainment that no longer exists ... and will perhaps never return. Is it any wonder this magnificent studio was nicknamed one of the dream palaces on our planet?

On one particular day while working with Lucille, we learned something about Jack Donahue we'd never suspected. He had one helluva temper ... a violent one. Time has dimmed and erased the particular cause, but something Lucille did, didn't, or wouldn't do, ticked him off. Had it been one of us four guys, he could easily have yelled at us and gotten it off his chest and out of his system. But because it was the star who'd done the offending deed, he was forced to accept it and say nothing. We became very aware of his attitude when we saw him clench his fists, walk suddenly and quickly to the back of the hall and with all the force that was in him, strike the wall. His right hand shot out as if to kill an opponent, hitting the cement like a bullet from a rifle. Seconds later, blood streaked slowly toward the floor like legs of an octopus. Cursing under his breath and grasping his right hand in his left, I watched him clench his teeth so hard I thought his jaw would surely break. At the same moment, he turned, disappeared through the door and headed toward the hospital adjacent to the rehearsal hall.

The four of us were speechless and turned toward Lucille. For one long moment her eyes remained in one of those wide open startled looks. Then as quickly as it happened, she did one of her famous double blinks, walked slowly across the hall and stopped in front of us. Leaning toward us, like she was about to share the secret of the ages, she said in a voice which could have been heard at the auto gate, "Jeeze! You guys know what? That guy has one helluva temper!"

The next morning during my entire trolley ride my thoughts were filled with nothing but a series of question marks. How were we supposed to act? What would we do or say? Those answers refused to come ... until I opened the door of Rehearsal Hall B and there in the very center of the hall, alone except for a young white-jacketed male nurse standing attentively behind a wheel chair, was our dear Lucille. She was seated woefully in the chair with one arm completely bandaged in a cast held in place by a sling. Also, one leg was solidly bound to the knee in bloodstained bandages, which on closer observation, had obviously been the handiwork of the wardrobe and makeup department. As if this wasn't enough, a large white Band-aid had been plastered across one cheek.

I was the only other person in the hall at the moment and there was absolutely no sound. Dead silence. Lucille's face was blank as she stared directly ahead ...into my eyes. The attendant mimicked her expression for what seemed endless minutes. Finally, the quiet was broken by the timely arrival of the other three guys who stopped dead in their tracks as Lucille nudged the attendant. Reacting slowly, he removed a rather large hand-painted sign, hidden until now by a robe thrown across the victim's lap. The sign was carefully handed to the pitiful creature, who lifted it high into the air for all to see. In large black print were the words: I WORK FOR JACK DONAHUE.

Meanwhile, for the balance of Thursday, our darling Lucille was pushed by her attendant from one end of the studio to the other, showing off her injuries and distress wherever she went. Even the huge sound stages with red lights blinking at the doors failed to stop the Wheelchair Duo. She winningly spoke to the guards whose primary duty was to protect closed sets. Everywhere, there was nothing but laughter and deep sympathy as the drama continued to reflect the attitude of stars and those surrounding them. On that particular day, MGM became a temporary nursing home and support group for a star forced to work for a "monster."

When lunch time rolled around, the four of us accompanied Lucille to her special table in the commissary. Helping to promote the illusion of all that had happened, we agreed with all reports she invented as the day progressed. Word spread throughout offices everywhere, creating interest from other stars, directors and producers, as well as members of wardrobe and makeup, grips, electricians, carpenters and stagehands. Eventually the publicity department sent photographers to cover the scene, resulting in almost an entire day of interruptions.

This was Thursday. The temper tantrum had happened on Wednesday and we didn't see our Mr. Tough Guy again until the following Monday. By that time, the swelling had reduced sufficiently and he appeared with only a rather bulky bandage to cover his self-inflicted wound, which all of us properly ignored.

CHAPTER FOUR

Reflections

For the sake of chronological authenticity, we now need to do a flashback to my arrival in Hollywood, along with a summary of exactly what led me to becoming a contract dancer for seven glorious years at Metro Goldwyn Mayer Studios.

Looking back through time to a period even before my teen years, and long before I learned about the birds and the bees, I was madly in love with such stars as Billie Dove, Clara Bow, Jean Harlow, and a few others including Anna May Wong. I believed that somehow, someday, I would join them in Hollywood. That dream continued to quietly grow, there in my equally quiet little hometown in Idaho (population: 2,000) until finally, after two years of college, I convinced my understanding parents that I needed to leave the provincial life and head for the bright lights of Hollywood.

With no further ado I packed a bag, and with my parents' concerned blessing, hitched a ride on a vegetable truck belonging to one of my father's farmer friends, and headed for a new life. The rough and tumble ride was little more than a way of getting from here to there, until we drove into an area I suddenly recognized as an environment completely foreign to my small town awareness. As we passed through San Bernardino and Riverside, the feeling I had was akin to being as close to Heaven as one could get and still be here on Earth.

I recall rolling down the window of the truck and leaning as far out as possible, trying my best to somehow become more a part of it all. Yes, all, for it seemed almost too good to be true ... It was then that I was sure what I'd done had been the right thing. This would be the turning point of my life. Hollywood held a far greater promise for me now than when I was tucked safely away in the security of my hometown. I'd dared to leave the cocoon, and now I knew why I was here, even before I completely unfolded my newfound wings.

Because I knew exactly why I'd come to Hollywood at age 20, it didn't take long to put down roots and begin to cultivate them. Not unusual for anyone in my situation was the very real necessity to get out and find employment. I needed to assure myself I was serious about making this my new and permanent place.

Jobs over the next couple of years consisted of working as a parking lot attendant, a soda jerk, theatre usher, delivery boy for a small market, general sales clerk, florist employee, and ceramist for the internationally recognized Sascha Brastoff, whose work was sponsored by one of the Rockerfeller's. This last job proved far superior to any of the others, and gave me insight into a creative field I'd not known before. The timing was right and I was allowed to learn nearly every phase of the business.

Cordially
Jean Harlow

Jean Harlow

Anna May Wong

I ended up as chief inspector on the final assembly line. It was fascinating in much the same way working for Mr. Rex, famous New York designer of ladies' chapeaux and the fabulous Adrian, former designer for top stars at MGM would be for me years later.

Eventually, I decided it was time to put my money where my mouth was. My father had just arrived from Idaho for a first visit. He wanted to be sure I was doing what my letters had claimed since my arrival in the "Magic Kingdom." He also wanted to be sure I wasn't living in the City of Sin. Soon satisfied it was not the latter; he accompanied me to the Faulkner Studios where I hoped to enroll as a student of the incomparable Adolph Bolm of the Imperial Russian Ballet.

Bolm had recently come to America to escape the difficulties of his war-torn homeland. He was a premier character dancer, and was equal to Nijinsky, Pavlova, Danilova and Krassovska in talent. What I was not aware of when we walked into the office was that one did not simply sign on the dotted line and show up for class next day. Each potential student must first be interviewed by Mr. Bolm and pass his personal requirements before being accepted.

We were aware that it was nearly lunch time and Mr. Bolm would soon be free to speak with us. According to the secretary, if I passed the interview the first class would be without charge. A final decision would be made after Bolm had seen me work with other students. Dad failed completely to understand all of this, since it did not blend with his business sense as a successful pharmacist.

We were comfortably seated for only a few minutes when the door leading to the dressing rooms and main studio opened and a pleasant, yet obviously serious, gentleman stood before us. He spoke quietly in a rather thick but easily understood Russian accent. Dad and I stood up the moment Mr. Bolm entered the office, and the three of us spoke briefly and seriously, Bolm's eyes took in my entire body as well as each word and answer to his questions. Then, as quietly and quickly as he'd entered

Tom Brown.

the room, he walked to the desk, spoke only a few words to the receptionist, and disappeared without so much as a backward glance. Five minutes later, we were once again out the door and standing on Hollywood Boulevard discussing where we would have lunch.

Schwab's Drug Store seemed a perfect place to eat, since it was a blend of Dad's business and a real opportunity to have a taste of good food, mixed with a bit of the excitement that made this little city different from any other in the world. As if to prove the point, we had no more than pulled on the handle of the door, than it opened effortlessly as two familiar figures brushed past us with a smile, walked to a waiting limo at the curb, and were whisked away. We both turned and stared, thinking that surely the two who had just passed were figments of our imaginations. One hour later, walking out the same door through which our so-called visions had passed, Dad was still not certain, which was which: Zsa Zsa or Eva? Oh, well, as far as I was concerned, a Gabor is a Gabor. Personally, I would've preferred seeing Tom Brown or Richard Cromwell.

Dad wasn't what one would call a movie-buff. Yet he was intrigued when I called his attention to the Garden of Allah, across the street from Schwab's. He was aware of both Gloria Swanson and Nazimova, both of whom helped make the place a part of the mystique and allure of so many Hollywood legends. Right now my thoughts were leaping ahead to 11 a.m. tomorrow morning, when I would take my first step toward the true reason for my being here.

The next day I was up earlier than usual, anticipating what might or might not happen between 11 and 12 o'clock. Before breakfast, I went through a long series of stretches and various exercises I knew would best prepare me for the big test I would soon take. I was more than a bit relieved when Dad announced he wouldn't be joining me, due to a phone call from an old friend now living in the area asking him to attend some sort of meeting.

Richard and Norman became special friends the very first time they met.

Richard Cromwell

I prepared rehearsal clothes in a special bag I'd purchased after leaving Schwab's the day before, and caught a bus which would take me to the studio with only one transfer. I'd been fortunate enough on my first day in Hollywood to find a wonderful apartment in Laurel Canyon, which suited my individual taste and needs in every way. Even though its location meant walking approximately a mile in order to reach Hollywood Boulevard seemed more of a plus than a minus.

I was accepted by Mr. Bolm and enrolled as a regular member of this particular class. Later I ended up dancing at the Hollywood Bowl (less than a year from this time); in an evening of music and ballet, which climaxed with the exciting and technical variations choreographed by Bolm for *Prince Igor, The Polovtsian Dances*. Strangely enough, my true debut in major theatre, later proved to be the same music for similar routines in my first film four years later.

Other famous dancers and choreographers were making their homes in the Hollywood and Beverly Hills area at this time as well. Stories relating to those with whom I studied and worked would be sufficient for writing. In order to give the reader at least some understanding as to just why I was able to qualify for a very special place at MGM in a rather short period of time, I must at least mention certain names of those who became an integral part of my training.

From Bolm I moved on to study with Serge Oukrainsky, one of the partners of the great Pavlova. Before leaving him, I was fortunate to participate in the writing and editing of his book, *My Two Years with Anna Pavlova*. From there I moved on to study with the modern dancer, Lester Horton, followed by Eduardo Cansino (father of Rita Hayworth), then Devi Dja, internationally recognized Balinese and Javanese dancer, and Jack Cole, modern stylist in this form of dance. It was Jack who choreographed dances for the movie version of *Kismet,* starring Marlene Dietrich just prior to my arrival at MGM. He moved to Columbia Pictures when Bob Alton took over the reins at MGM.

It was a time of many changes, all of which paved the way for the great era of movie musicals. Through Jack Cole, I met America's First Lady of the Dance, Ruth St. Denis, with whom I studied and danced, becoming an instructor at her studio.

In addition, yes, here was another individual whose story could add several chapters to this book. Last, but far from least, were my days, weeks, months, and years of working with the one-and-only Eleanor Powell. Ellie and I, during the time she was married to Glenn Ford, became like brother and sister, particularly during a two year span when I became her choreographer for a children's show at NBC which won five Emmy Awards.

Ruth St. Denis in "Tagore Poem," 1929. St. Denis was a pioneer of contemporary dance.

Norman in "Ali Baba and the Forty Thieves," with Alexandra Bokhara, center. She later became one of the Mack Sennett Bathing Beauties and assumed the name of Mimi La Marr. She was married to Norman Borine in 1940 in Los Angeles.

Photo by Juan Marquna.

CHAPTER FIVE

Nijinsky's Sister Opens Door

The name Nico Charisse was not exactly a household name until he had been married for some time to one of his students, Cyd Finklea, a young Jewish girl from Texas. While studying at his studio with the great Bronislava Nijinska, I was more than fortunate to have her recommend me to the casting office at Universal Studios for my first movie job in a film starring Maria Montez, Jon Hall, and Turhan Bey. When I learned the film would be titled *Ali Baba and the Forty Thieves,* I was suddenly not only grateful to be studying with such a distinguished personality from the Imperial Russian Ballet, cognizant of all I'd gained through the classic techniques of my other two Russian instructors and choreographers, Balm and Oukrainsky. That particular morning, following the lesson, I lingered a bit in the dressing-room, and then stopped at the desk to thank Madame Nijinska (through her husband-interpreter) for her kindness in giving my name to Universal in answer to their call.

The walk up La Brea Avenue, the short bus ride along Sunset, and the long walk up Laurel Canyon to my hideaway seemed far shorter than ever before today. Several times I caught myself humming or singing the words to "Over the Rainbow." Though it would be several months before I'd be signing "The Big Contract," I somehow felt that tomorrow I would take a step in that direction. And, of course, I did.

Arriving at Universal the next morning, it seemed every male dancer in Hollywood and New York had come to compete for the twelve openings. Not only was this my first experience of auditioning in a real honest-to-God movie studio, but was my first real audition of any kind. Bolm had been choreographer for the Hollywood Bowl appearance, so I hadn't had to audition. I'll admit to being nervous, who wouldn't be? Just being in a major studio was enough to create excitement.

We were told how and where to sign in, and then everyone milled about in groups while we waited to be called. The only thing that gave me a bit of comfort was the knowledge that somewhere among this group of 150 to 200 hopefuls were two other guys from Nijinska's class with whom I was at least familiar. The rest were total strangers. I didn't know until later that the two from our class were among the first to be auditioned, simply because they were already members of the Screen Actor's Guild. Both were accepted as two of the twelve destined to get jobs.

I watched as assistants to the choreographer began dividing everyone into groups of 16 (two lines of 8) to perform a variety of basic steps and combinations. This was followed by more complicated movements specifically and technically Russian in style.

When my turn finally arrived, I couldn't be certain if having been recommended by Nijinska helped or not, but I was selected for the final tryout. That's when the perspiration really began to run. From the total original group, the choreographer picked only 20. All the others were thanked and excused.

Norman, pictured at the back in the center, enjoyed working on this Columbia Studios picture, other than the hot floor on his nearly bare feet.

1943

1322-195

My stomach was suddenly filled with butterflies all doing flip-flops and loop-the-loops as we were auditioned in groups of 6, then 4, then 2 before the reading of the list of those selected. I didn't know whether to laugh, cry, scream, or collapse at the sound of my name being included in the twelve.

I have total recall of a tremendous sense of elation while passing through the studio gates and heading for the big red street car. I dropped my dime into the box next to the motorman knowing that in less than 24 hours I'd be rehearsing for my very first movie.

Actually, it wasn't quite that simple. Though I'd made the audition, there was a complication not anticipated. Even being recommended by Nijinska, there was the technicality of not being a member of the Screen Actor's Guild. To have the job, I was required to be a member. For a time it seemed they might decide to select a replacement who was already a member from the audtion list.

Finally, after a series of phone calls, it was agreed the studio would accept a written letter from Nijinska, after which I would qualify as a full-fledged member. Meanwhile, I was given a temporary card, allowing me to work until the letter arrived and I had received a permanent Guild card. All of this took more than an hour in the casting office, so I missed the preliminary warm-up and beginning series of combinations. However, I was in. I'd made it and I thanked the universe.

During the first day's rehearsal I actually had moments when I wished I hadn't passed the audition. The steps and combinations of Russian techniques proved so strenuous and difficult I could barely climb aboard the red car at the end of the afternoon. The next morning was even worse. When I awoke, I was certain I wouldn't be able to get out of bed, much less reach that first step of the streetcar or get off and walk to the studio. The very thought of a second day of rehearsal seemed absolutely out of the question. However, after a long hot shower and substantial breakfast followed by a series of

Norman was occasionally loaned out to every other major studio to appear with top stars during the magical period of great musicals which will never come again. Here Yvonne De Carlo sits with Tilly Losch, coreographer, at Universal Pictures. This was the first studio to engage Norman in his unusual and colorful career.

1946

stretches and deep-knee-bends, I began to believe I might somehow make it. I'd just think about one-step at a time. Even then, it was difficult to believe I could be so stiff and sore when I'd been regularly attending advanced ballet classes three times a week for nearly two years. After a few days, the muscles became used to the new style and the new steps that were combined with leaps and turns and were required during these extremely difficult workouts.

At the end of five weeks of rehearsal, I was amazed to find the actual shooting of the number was pleasant and almost effortless. I must explain the "almost" by telling you that the entire sequence was filmed outdoors during some usual summer heat. The setting was the courtyard of a Persian Palace. Generally, when they depicted an outdoor location, the scene was duplicated inside a sound stage with special backdrops and props realistic enough to convince most moviegoers it was indeed outside. This was not the case for this scene.

While Maria Montez and Jon Hall were seated on a sort of throne watching us, shaded by artificial Palm trees, we were burning up... sweating with our feet screaming for help. Why? Because what appeared to be genuine Cossack boots made of leather were, in reality, nothing but simulated leather designed to fit over our thin ballet slippers. The effect was convincing, but dancing on a linoleum floor made to look like marble outdoors in the hot summer sun for extended takes, was anything but pleasant. Of course our burning, frustrated feet no doubt reflected in our facial expressions, all adding to the desired intensity of the characters we portrayed.

Each time the director called "cut," we warriors with swords wasted no time in heading for the side of the set to stand on thick wringing-wet mops, prepared for us each time we heard the welcome word. This is exactly where we remained until we again heard the familiar voice over the loudspeaker call out: "Okay dancers, take your places, please" ... followed by a polite: "Miss Montez ... Mr. Hall ... are you ready?" Then a slight pause, before the final: "Thank you ... all right, everybody ... camera ... action!" Again, we were back on the hot fake marble floor, dancing and mentally awaiting the next break.

No doubt, many readers will recall the shock relating to the untimely death of our lovely and beautiful star, Maria Montez who, years later was strangely electrocuted as she talked on a telephone while in the bathtub in her Paris apartment. Looking back now, I begin to wonder if my attitude toward her would have in any way been altered during the weeks we worked together if somehow I could intuitively have known such a thing would happen. Perhaps. Perhaps not! Time and circumstances often alter our day to day thoughts and opinions. As with Joan Crawford and others of bygone days, she was in every way the epitome of a real honest and true movie star. To me, working in my very first film, that's what I expected and that's what she was. I was not disappointed.

We spent three weeks rehearsing the one big dance number, plus another two full weeks shooting it. During the entire time I felt truly comfortable and at home there on the set in this "dream come true" major studio.

Heading out on the last day of work, I was aware of a rather strange and empty feeling in my stomach ... but it wasn't there for long. Nearing the casting office, someone beckoned to me from inside, motioning for me to come in. Thirty seconds later I was informed there would be a big audition the following morning for Tilly Losch, a choreographer brought from London, who'd be creating a production number for Yvonne De Carlo in a new film, *Song of Schehrezade*. Though it was an open call, those of us from *Ali Baba* were told we would be on a special list for the audition. Once again my spirits soared as I turned and made my way through the door toward the big red car ... I was filled with hope.

Those hopes were temporarily dampened next morning as I arrived inside the studio and discovered, just as before, a large crowd consisting of more than two hundred dancers, both male and female, with one hope in common ... to get the job. My heart took a nosedive when an acquaintance informed me they were looking for only four guys and four girls. To make it worse, I learned the number was to be a Spanish cape dance. With only one film to my credit and strictly classical ballet as my only background, I grew uneasy. Common sense, however, came to my rescue as I told myself that technically, Spanish dancing could be no more difficult than what I'd gone through in *Ali Baba.* So, I mentally tightened my belt and accepted the fact that I had as much chance as anyone. Yes, I decided, I'd simply change my attitude and my style and do it in Spanish.

This was near the beginning of what would later prove to have been the grand and glorious era of giant musicals on the silver screen. At this point it seemed every dancer in Hollywood was looking for work. The audition took place over a three day period, and as before we were first called together in groups of twenty-five. We stood in lines and attempted to follow what we were shown by the assistant choreographer who performed simple basic steps and combinations to the beat and melodies coming from an old grand piano nearly hidden in one corner of the large soundstage.

Tilly first explained what she wanted, while a secretary made notes to keep track of dancers who might or might not end up as one of the chosen few. During the uncertainty of it all, the star, Yvonne, sat quietly in a nearby director's chair which bore her name in large letters across the back, occasionally conferring with Tilly relating to some dance step or a particular dancer. Time passed until, as lunch hour arrived, they had seen each group of 25 and all of us were told to relax and return in one hour. Most of the group were old-timers who drifted off here and there to gather in groups and enjoy the

Tilly Losch had originally been brought from London to do the infamous dance atop a saloon bar in the film, "Duel in the Sun, "starring Jennifer Jones and Gregory Peck. She was retained to choreograph the cape dance with Yvonne De Carlo.

snack lunch they'd brought. The rest headed toward the commissary or relaxed over nothing more than a cup of coffee or thermos of cool water.

Exactly one hour later, we were together on the sound stage where the number would be filmed. The afternoon was similar to the morning session, differing only in size of groups performing the tryout combinations. We began with 12 at a time rather than 25, with each grouping becoming successively smaller. At the close of day more than half the group had been dismissed. Those remaining, including me, were given a callback for the next morning.

Needless to say, my evening at home was spent primarily going over as many steps and combinations as I could recall. I was attempting to add more strength and style to my steps than I'd had during the tryouts. At bedtime, I felt again that a hand was guiding me and I'd be okay. I repeated over and over: "I know I can do it. I know I can do it. I know I can do it."

In my imagination I could see Tilly and Yvonne, and I felt their eyes watching me and smiling … as I went right on dancing.

At the end of the next day, having switched from groups of six to four, I was one of those asked to report for the final selection the next morning. By now, the group had shrunk from more than 200 to 16. Of this group, only three were Caucasian … the rest were either Mexican or Spanish, with dark hair. I was the only blonde.

Need I say I spent the evening exactly as I had twenty-four hours earlier? Shortly before noon the next day, we had completed the workouts. Eight names were selected. Four guys and four gals. All Latin types except one … me. At that point, I could hardly restrain the tears. Not tears of surprise, but of total relief. Moreover, I was grateful.

I'd passed the test ... I was the only non-Latin type picked from more than 200 dancers ... I was going to be in a Spanish cape dance with Yvonne De Carlo and her co-Star, Jean-Pierre Aumont. I was elated. I could hardly believe that I'd arrived at Universal to work in one film (my first), and now I remained for a second.

Tilly Losch had originally been brought from London to do the infamous dance atop a saloon bar in the film, *Duel in the Sun*, starring Jennifer Jones and Gregory Peck. Due to its tremendous success, she was retained to choreograph our exciting cape dance with Yvonne.

Though my classic ballet training from Bolm, Oukrainsky, and Nijinska had included a certain amount of character dancing, it was not until some time later that I added Spanish techniques learned from the then well-known Eduardo Cansino, father of Rita Hayworth. At times, the new challenges were a bit much, but by struggling and somewhat bluffing my way along for the first few days as we set the routine, I managed not to show my limitations. As the days grew in number, so did my confidence. By the time we were twirling the giant bull fighter capes, I discovered this experience was also new to the three companions with whom I was working. Fortunately, both Tilly and her assistant willingly spent countless hours patiently showing us exactly what was required to create the desired effect. They managed to make all of us appear convincingly professional as we twirled our capes and shouted "Olé!" with mucho gusto.

These were the days before such things as limited budgets and no overtime were included in studio vocabulary. Often while shooting we'd go past regular quitting time by only 10 or 15 minutes still receive overtime pay. We weren't allowed to pass the deadline even by two minutes without being paid a full quarter-check extra. This wasn't only for the talent, it included full payment for every single individual on the set. Time and money seemed unimportant. What mattered was getting the job done right ... regardless of cost. It wasn't until the beginning of the '50s that studios began to tighten the reins ... the year, which brought a close to my contract with MGM, thus leaving me to savor memories of a time never to be repeated.

One day shortly after being selected for this particular cape twirling job, I was stopped by someone at casting and told it might be wise to put a dark rinse on my hair, lest our choreographer have second thoughts about having a blond Spaniard performing in the number. I stopped at a Thrifty Drug Store on Hollywood Boulevard on my way home and purchased what I felt to be the correct bottle of hair coloring. After dinner the same evening I read the directions and applied the dye as directed, then dried my hair and hit the sack.

Needless to say, what looked back at me in the mirror next morning was a total shock. Never having experienced life as a brown-haired person, I felt I should perhaps change my name to Fernando. It would certainly give more believability to my performance in the Fandango. As it happened, my own reactions were not much different from those at the studio. When I arrived at casting a few hours later, I was asked to show my ID Card before they were convinced it was really me. Even the individual who had suggested the haircolor change was amazed with what appeared to be a complete and total personality switch. Moments later when arriving for rehearsal, people naturally observed my presence, but no one spoke. Not a word. My usual greeting provoked nothing more than a nod or half-smile, and I began to wonder just what the hell was going on. What could I have possibly done to cause this sudden lack of acknowledgment?

Wardrobe had not realized it would require two additional days of rehearsal to allow us to execute the flourish and twirling effects needed for all the intricate choreography Tilly had created. Norman center, behind Yvonne.

P3-108

Feeling completely ostracized, it wasn't until Tilly walked over to me and informed me that visitors were not allowed on the set that I realized the effectiveness of my unintended disguise. Then, with a subtle sense of humor, she made an elaborate introduction to the dancers. She made a big production of emphasizing that the new dancer replacing Norman had been fully rehearsed in the entire dance, which has been choreographed thus far. During this farce, I continued to inwardly be amazed that one small bottle of Clairol could make such an effective outer change. I also felt relieved that I was now in no danger of being replaced.

During rehearsals, we used heavy black satin capes, unaware that at some point we would experience certain changes to create a more realistic effect. A day or two before actual shooting, wardrobe arrived on the set with the real stuff, letting us know that until now we had just been playing with blank bullets. What we saw were not the single-fabric capes, but double reversible capes, black on one side and a strikingly brilliant electric blue on the other ... weighing exactly twice as much. Tilly was obviously pleased with the effect, but what wardrobe had not realized was that it would require two additional days of rehearsal to allow us to execute the flourish and twirling effects needed for all the intricate choreography Tilly had created.

Shooting plans suddenly changed and began three days later and ended in exactly two weeks. On the last day, we became aware we'd be working into half time. Prior to our last shot, which would most definitely take several hours to complete, the studio caterers arrived and set up an elaborate meal right on the set, giving us time to rest without changing our entire costumes or going to the commissary.

Since it was our final day, as opposed to simply another overtime occasion, the entire set was in a festive mood, causing us to barely make deadline that evening. Following the delicious and extended meal, a bit of fresh makeup was all that was required before returning to the sounds of "All right, everybody on the Set ... Quiet, please. Lights! Camera! Action!"

Then suddenly it was over. Ended. My second film! But far from my last!

As a matter of fact, another surprise is worthy of report, albeit not in detail. Once again, the very day on which we completed the film with Yvonne, I was notified by the casting office that they would like me to remain for a third film. They'd already checked with the choreographer and learned it wouldn't be necessary for me to attend the audition, since they were definitely aware of my work. Naturally I was happy to learn I would once again not be leaving the studio as expected; an extra bonus was added when I learned who the star of the film was — none other than Susanna Foster! Though I didn't have a crush on her, I truly loved her voice and was excited to have an opportunity to work with her in *The Climax.*

Aside from the fact I have never seen the film, my memory more than half a century later refuses to recall anything special pertaining to the number. There does remain some feeling of pleasure at having spent a number of weeks rehearsing and shooting the production number with Susanna and 20 or 30 other male dancers. In addition, in admitting the fact, I experience a sense of confusion while being aware how perfectly my mind recalls experiences pertaining to other persons and events within the identical period. Perhaps I shall be excused when expressing it this way: not all flowers in a beautiful garden claim equal attention from either our sense of sight or smell. Might we not say the same about the stars, regardless of whether they emanate from Heaven or Hollywood?

Betty
Hutton

CHAPTER SIX

Betty Hutton ... Angel in Disguise

The first studio I worked for was Universal, where I worked on three films in a row. I ended up at Paramount Pictures after someone in Universal's casting department gave them my name. Paramount was looking for dancers to appear with one of their big stars, Betty Hutton. I was more than happy for the opportunity to work in another film.

At this time I was living in a little house on Vine Street, approximately one mile from Paramount, so it was an easy trek, especially in contrast to the hour trolley ride I'd been making to Universal during the past three months. Little did I suspect that this would be the key that would soon open a magic door and lead to steady work for me for years to come.

Upon arriving at Paramount I found myself in the company of nearly seventy-five dancers, including those with whom I'd worked at Universal. Even knowing some of us had been recommended prior to

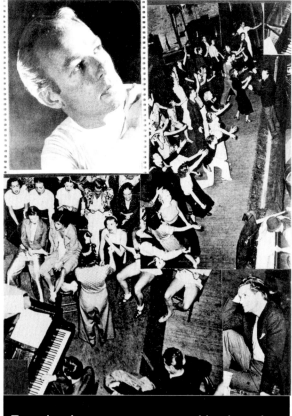

Typical audition scene experienced by the author. Prior to being awarded a seven-year dance contract in 1943 by MGM's top choreographer, Robert Alton, lower right.

the audition, I became uneasy upon discovering they were only planning to select four boys and four girls. I was still too new at the game to understand that I was one of those already chosen, and the audition was only a technicality necessary to fulfill the rules of the Screen Actors Guild.

Billy Daniels, the young choreographer who auditioned us, was the lover of Mitch Leisen who was one of Paramount's biggest directors, and the one who would be directing the Betty Hutton film, *Incendiary Blonde.* Billy put us through our paces, requiring us to follow his combinations of tap, jazz, and ballet. Then he had his assistant read off the names of the eight chosen to remain, before thanking everyone for coming while at the same time excusing them. Moments later, as the hall became nearly empty, Billy walked over to our little group (yes, I'd made it), and introduced himself, at the same time asking our names and shaking hands before giving us our call for the next day. That was it. We were dismissed, and I was happy.

Our call was for 10 a.m. that first morning, and the hours before lunch time were spent becoming familiar with the music and lyrics to an oldie I'd been familiar

Norman appears to the right behind Betty Hutton in "Incendiary Blonde," wearing one of the many feathered costumes of his career.
1945

with growing up: *Oh, By Jingo.* The experimentation Billy made with dance steps and combinations were nearly as crazy as the lyrics themselves, bringing a lot of laughs and remarks from all of us as we worked through them. Billy warned us, however, not to take them too seriously because our star, who was not attending rehearsal that particular day, would make many of the final decisions. Little did we know how true his statement would prove to be.

Still a somewhat naive small town Idaho boy, I got a crash-course in "How To Express Ideas, Thoughts and Emotions By Using Only Four-Letter Words," when Miss Betty arrived to watch us run through what we'd accomplished on our first day. Immediately, it was "Jesus H. Christ, what's this all about ... and what the shit are we trying to do ..." etc., etc. until my up to then virgin ears gradually became numb to at least most of her remarks. As the day wore on and we began singing and dancing for longer periods of time, our star seemed a bit less formidable. Walking home later in the day, I found myself chuckling about some of the things she'd said or done throughout the afternoon.

Returning through the Paramount Pictures arch the next morning brought forth anticipation about what might happen on this second day with the shocking personality I'd encountered the day before. In citing an example now, let me again remind the reader that this is 1943, when the garment industry had very recently released a rather daring product for women which they labeled pedal pushers.

It so happened two of the four girls working with us showed up wearing them for rehearsal that particular morning. About 10:30, La Hutton walked into the room and then stopped dead in her tracks. At the top of her voice, while looking directly at the two girls, she let out a shriek, followed by the words: "Jesus H. Christ, what in hell is that?" She pointed directly at the outfits the girls were wearing, and then went on: "And where did they come from, the Goodwill Store? They are really shitty!"... All of which did not go over too well with either of the girls, inasmuch as they were far from what anyone could or would refer to as slouches. One of the two snapped back at our star: "Jealousy will get you nowhere, Miss Hutton, and it really doesn't matter, since your ass wouldn't fit into them, anyhow."

Needless to say, upon returning from lunch, we were minus one female dancer. The next morning we became acquainted briefly with her replacement, and though the morning moved along rather smoothly, I smelled a rat. Though I wasn't aware of what caused the feeling, immediately following lunch, we learned the validity of my hunch. Not only did our Incendiary Blonde fail to show up for the rest of the afternoon, but our rehearsal hall was entirely girl-less, leaving only Billy and the four of us guys to continue a few new combinations.

We continued this way through Thursday, and were told we need not report to the studio until our usual time on Monday morning. This, because of our weekly contracts, meant we would still be entitled to a full week's pay. We were delighted to celebrate the event, each in his own way. As for me, I was up early the next morning and heading for a long day at Santa Monica Beach.

The following Monday morning we became aware that our Madame Queen had not only frowned upon the stylish peddle pushers, but upon all the girls as well. "Those dames," she began, "were real shit heads. The number will be better off without them." She was obviously assured of our approval when she finished off with, "Besides, it will be more fun with just you four guys …. so let's get on with it." And we did.

From that time forward, it was smooth sailing. As Billy had suspected on our first day, major portions of the dance combinations we'd rehearsed were ignored and now, a week later, we began almost totally anew. We rehearsed the crazy lyrics to *Oh, By Jingo* (Oh, by gee, by gosh, by gum, by Jove…) until we could sing them backwards and forward, making change after change in the dance as we went along. We did this step by step, according to Betty's final approval. Unlike Jack Donahue, Billy Daniels was extremely easy-going and flexible, and not the least bit bothered if we had to try six or eight versions of any particular combination until Betty was satisfied.

The four of us had now begun to enjoy the whole experience of working with this character who was such a far cry from the personalities we'd encountered at Universal. Something else new to us became a sort of bonus. Betty, of course, being the star for the film, was shooting dialogue scenes simultaneously with our rehearsals, so consequently it necessitated her absence from the single number in which we were involved. Ordinarily in a musical film, all dialogue is shot either prior to or after the musical portion, therefore avoiding an arrangement like we were enjoying. In other words, once the routine had been set and Betty was involved in dialogue shots, we were allowed to come in late or take off early, depending on the schedule set up by the director. By the end of our second week, we were aware that the time at Paramount would be a fun six weeks, if not longer, as opposed to the originally planned four. Today, such events seldom occur. In our time frame, any such change in plans was simply and casually a part of running a major studio.

My next new experience began immediately following our first costume fitting, when I found myself being invited for lunch at the well-known Lucy's Restaurant located across Melrose Avenue opposite the Paramount gates. It certainly wasn't a place frequented by anyone not upper echelon of the studio. To an average worker it was thought of primarily as the place where the stars dined. The invitation came as a complete surprise through none other than our Incendiary Blonde. However, it didn't take long to figure who had instigated it and was picking up the tab ... none other than well-known costume designer, Raoul Du Bois. He'd recently been brought in from the New York world of theatre to execute wardrobe primarily for the big musical, *Lady in the Dark*, starring Ginger Rogers.

Entering Lucy's with Betty that noon, we were escorted through the elegant and dimly lit restaurant to a somewhat secluded linen-draped table, which suggested our arrival was not exactly unexpected. This little clue was brought to my attention by the three (not two) crystal water glasses placed properly with each set-up. A small but beautiful corsage had been added to the center one of the three.

An added surprise was that someone was seated at one of the place settings. A man, not familiar to me, and not much older than me occupied the seat. He stood up, reached for Betty's hand, and then bowed as he kissed it. Until now, I wasn't certain whether he was aware of my presence, but the feeling quickly changed as he turned and performed his slight bow to me, at the same time speaking my name in greeting. *Well,* I thought to myself, *he was apparently expecting me as well as Betty, since he knew my name, so I guess whatever this is all about is okay.*

He didn't kiss my hand, and I was relieved. The three of us seated ourselves, and Betty smiled as she made an informal introduction. I immediately felt more relaxed. Inwardly, I felt a bit uncomfortable at meeting such an important New York stage designer, especially after learning he created both sets and costumes. I was, of course, already aware that he was quite famous. As his noticeably blue eyes scanned my face and gave me a polite but definite once over, I smiled at his obvious approval. I noticed at the same time that anyone seeing the three of us might easily have assumed we were members of one family. We were all blondes with blue eyes.

I have no recollection of our conversation, nor of the food we ate, but what is still strong in my memory was the sudden change in feelings I began to have toward the star we were sitting with. Until now, I'd seen her as a totally outrageous and raucous character. Somehow, she was no longer the dingbat image I'd carried around in my mind. Yes, she was still rather looney, but now she also seemed warm and almost lovable.

Raoul on the other hand, was quietly the same, yet ever so different. Reserved, polite, intelligent and gentle, in many ways he appeared almost childlike in his appreciation of Betty's blatant but now toned down humor. I couldn't help wondering, throughout the beautiful meal, just what part of her coarseness was real and how much was simply for effect ... an act for getting attention. Whatever the answer, I more and more began to see her in a new and different light. It felt good sitting there with my two new friends in this lovely and comfortable place away from the rest of the world.

Following lunch, as the three of us walked again beneath the wrought iron Paramount Pictures arch, there were far different thoughts running through my mind than the ones I would experience later, on my own personal Yellow Brick Road at MGM.

Raoul bid a temporary farewell to Betty and me as he headed for the wardrobe department. We turned our footsteps in the opposite direction toward the rehearsal hall. I cannot deny the feelings that swept across me only moments later when one of our four sarcastically inquired, "... and how was the food over where the elite meet to eat, Mr. Borine?" We were in the midst of rehearsal then, and as he passed by again only seconds later he added, " ... and do please turn all the way around so I can see if any of the stardust rubbed off on you."

The remarks were audible only to me, as Betty was having more difficulty than usual with the particular combination in which we were involved. She was completely unaware of the snide comments. I just wondered how such information could travel so fast.

Naturally, it didn't take a psychic to figure out that I'd been singled out by Betty to become a permanent luncheon companion at Lucy's for the duration of our Paramount engagement. Thus the threesome of Betty, Raoul, and Norman became a regular grouping each day for lunch, and were often spotted at one of the elite Hollywood night spots like Ciro's, the Brown Derby, the Mocambo or the Florentine Gardens.

In the days to follow, comments from my three co-dancers grew more frequent. One of them was a close friend, so there was no problem there. He took it in stride. The other two seemed to have a problem allowing me the freedom to associate with my new friends. Apparently they felt I was stepping out of my class.

What they soon discovered, and what proved simply too, too much was the fact that following a recent visit to the Florentine Gardens, I was picked up at the front gate of the studio each day and driven home by Raoul's chauffeur. Actually, since I was not a born show-off, I didn't really give it much thought. I just appreciated Betty's friendship and Raoul's thoughtfulness. His hours being longer than ours were, he simply sent the chauffeur, knowing I would otherwise walk home. On several occasions, particularly when the big secret was discovered, the two guys would make a point of reaching the front gate just ahead of me, and then watch the chauffeur drive me off into the sunset.

Earlier, I mentioned Betty having difficulty with a certain step in our routine. Actually, it was a rather long series of somewhat tricky steps, though not technically difficult. During shooting, all of us discovered that the colorfully crazy costumes dreamed up by Raoul did not particularly help the situation ... the costumes were made up of primarily feathers, beads, and a very tight jock strap (not necessarily included in Betty's personal wardrobe, though very much in keeping with ours). Time has in no way dimmed the memory of particular eight-bar combination that required 22 takes before Mitch Leisen was satisfied and called, "Cut! Print!" Since we were near the end of the day, this small-unexpected screw-up cost the studio enough time to go into overtime, adding considerable dollars to every individual paycheck at the end of the week, regardless of where we were located on the symbolic studio totem pole.

We were to finish shooting on Friday, so during our "Farewell to Lucy's" luncheon on Thursday, Betty and Raoul suggested we have some sort of celebration that evening at the Florentine Gardens. It seemed especially appropriate when Betty reminded us there was a possibility we might even complete the last two shots today, due to a shift in plans by the director and cameraman.

Returning to the set and discussing things with Billy, we were in great spirits when we learned we would definitely be finished earlier than they had planned, even though one of the shots involved special props and unusual lighting. Perhaps due to our plans for the evening, I was totally minus the usual empty emotions ordinarily a part of leaving at the end of a film. Maybe the Universe was already whispering something in my ear that was soon to take place. Had I been even slightly aware of the message, the evening ahead would've seemed dull in comparison.

That evening, the driver jumped out of the car and greeted me politely as I walked from my little house to join Betty and Raoul in the back seat as we were whisked off to another magical evening. I felt like I was living one of the fairy tales I'd enjoyed reading as a child. Minutes later, we were seated at our favorite booth inside the fabulous restaurant, off in a corner where we could visit with minimum interruption.

On this particular evening the drinks and food seemed particularly good as we watched and listened to the band. Before and after the spectacular floorshow, Raoul and I took turns leading Betty onto the dance floor, where we were generally the center of attention because of our partner. She never failed to attract people to our table who politely asked for an autograph, or occasionally made a request for permission to be photographed with her. By this time my Idaho shyness was rapidly diminishing. I was at a point where I found myself actually enjoying being a part of the attention.

Whether it was the drinks or the music and elaborate floorshow, or a bit of each combined with the food and general celebration at having completed the fun dance number at the studio earlier in the day, we were in such a celebrating mood that we decided to order after dinner drinks and remain for the second show. While I was sipping a White Russian, which turned out to be both new and especially tasty to me, Raoul asked Betty and me if we would like to attend an unusual party the next evening at the home of a friend in Bel Air.

Betty, I soon discovered, was already acquainted with the friend and some of those who would be at his home. Raoul immediately responded to my somewhat blank look by explaining that it was being held at the home of Bob Alton, whom he and Betty had known in New York. He further informed me that MGM had recently brought Bob to the studio as their primary choreographer. It seems he had five major Broadway shows running at the same time, but because musicals were now the rage, they made him an offer he couldn't refuse.

Raoul assured me I'd enjoy the party planned for the next night because nearly all of those invited were young New York dancers who'd worked for Bob and had followed him to Hollywood, assured of a solid work schedule. Some of them had even left the show in which they were working, being completely sold on what he'd promised them. Yes, this was the '40s ... the time of the great musicals. And a dancer's pay in Hollywood was now better than anywhere in the world.

Here, now, with both Raoul and Betty at the Florentine Gardens, hearing an invitation to a sort of gathering still new to me, my mind became a confusion of thoughts and pictures. The decision was difficult. Then, from amidst the uncertainty came Betty's remark, "Hey, boy, what-cha got to lose? I'll be there, too, and we'll all have another great evening ... just like tonight."

As though rising from the surface of a pool, I shook my head, blinked, ordered another White Russian and replied, "OK, it's a deal."

Looking back, the following evening's events play out like a movie script. Ciro's was a convenient place for the three of us to meet, and I had arrived only a few moments before Raoul and Betty drove up beneath the mammoth neon sign. Betty leaned out the window, asking the young parking attendant if he'd seen me. He was familiar with the three of us because of our many visits to the club. Actually, I was only a short distance away, having just made a phone call from a nearby booth. The attendant approached the car, then turned and pointed in my direction. Climbing casually into the front seat beside Betty I smiled a farewell to the attendant, who told us to have a nice evening, and we drove away.

Approximately 20 minutes later we left Sunset Boulevard and turned right onto Bel Air Road. Three or four minutes later our car was parked along with many others occupying the wide curved driveway. We closed the doors behind us and walked toward the huge southern style mansion, complete with columns, that looked like something from *Gone With the Wind*. The manicured walkway wound through the scented garden and led us up a wide stairway onto a veranda. As we walked, we caught the strains of a familiar Broadway tune and the sounds of laughter.

The huge door opened in response to our ringing the bell. One of the guests immediately recognized Raoul and welcomed him with open arms. Betty was second in line, with me not far behind. I had a feeling of being *Alice in Wonderland*. Maybe it's just that I was suddenly looking for a rabbit-hole to jump down. For a moment I stood like one of the columns on the porch outside, though not feeling all that big or strong, and certainly not that grand. It was rather like walking into a brightly lit room after spending a very long time in the dark.

As my eyes began to focus, I felt a hand on my arm and heard a familiar voice saying, "I'm going to look for Bob. Betty is in the music room talking with some of her friends. Maybe you'd like to join some of the people in the kitchen, that's where the popcorn is." Raoul knew what I liked.

I followed my nose to an area to the left, making special effort to appear calm and casual. As I entered the room, still acting casual of course, it was as though someone in that kitchen was aware of my weakness for fresh, hot, buttered popcorn, which to this day can do more for me, temporarily, than anything else. From out of nowhere some friendly soul put a large ceramic bowl in my hand, accompanied by "help yourself" before disappearing into the group surrounding me. I followed the instructions and helped myself with no hesitation from a larger ceramic bowl filled with popcorn. I spent the next five minutes munching, allowing my eyes to move about the room and take in the beautiful girls and handsome men, all about my age, 26.

In the kitchen I continued to lean against the counter, look around the room, and eat ... and eat ... until my reverie was broken when Raoul appeared. He walked over to my side and quietly said, "Oh, I see you found him before I did."

My eyes widened, I glanced around, and then back at Raoul. "Found who?" Before he could reply, something clicked in my brain and my eyes went directly to the older man who was actually responsible for all the deliciousness I was feasting on. He also happened to own the beautiful home in which we were guests. Saying to myself, *Oh, and this must be Bob Alton*, I realized that he wasn't really so old after all. Of course, most of us were in our mid-twenties, and I assumed Bob was somewhere in that nebulous area of over forty...

Hearing the voice of his special New York friend, Bob looked up, relinquished his popping job to one of the guys standing nearby and walked over to extend a cordial greeting while looking me over with an experienced eye. "This must be Norman," he said, shaking my hand. His eyes were noticeably sharp and discerning as he added, "and how soon can you join us for work at MGM?"

Raoul had meant this to be a surprise for me. And it was. The obvious blank look on my face brought forth a statement from Bob, rather than a repetition of the question. "I'd like to have you come to the studio and work for me."

When I asked, "What picture are you doing?"

I got a momentary questioning expression from Bob before he quickly recovered and continued. "Actually, we're not doing anything right at the moment and it may be two or three weeks before we begin. But it doesn't matter, at least not to you, since you'll be under contract and paid just as though you were working."

His words and expression were so matter-of-fact that I felt stupid when I repeated his key word. "Contract?"

To this day I'm not sure how long I stood there looking at him before he suddenly got the picture and realized I didn't know what he was talking about. Deliberately tuning his back on Raoul, he came closer, putting one hand on my shoulder as he leaned to my ear. "It seems to me, Norman, that this character standing behind me didn't bother to tell you about my serious intentions." He turned, gave Raoul a comical wilting look before facing me again, and at the same time, in a loud stage whisper, said very clearly and deliberately so everyone in the kitchen could hear. "I, Robert Alton, now choreographer for MGM, do hereby announce that I would like you to appear at the studio as soon as possible for the purpose of signing a seven-year contract." His voice seemed to fade as he carefully took the empty popcorn bowl from my hand, walked over to the huge bowl someone had re-filled, then dipped mine into it, poured butter over it, salted it, and walked directly back to me, extending it as though it, in itself, were the contract.

I reached for the corn, aware of the words ringing in my ears: "… a contract … for the next seven years." At the exact moment the words went swirling through my mind, my hands reached out, only to let the bowl slip through my fingers. It landed on the floor, hitting at the same time as those unbelievable words repeated themselves in my mind, "…for the next seven years."

Jean Harlow, one of the author's favorites, in a studio portrait from "The Girl from Missouri."

CHAPTER SEVEN

20ᵀᴴ Century Fox Adventures

Admittedly, except for her performance in *The Misfits* also starring Clark Gable, Marilyn Monroe was never one of my favorite actresses. This in no way indicates I am putting her down. She was simply not my cup o' tea. Perhaps in many ways it was because as a teenager I had a big crush on Jean Harlow, and though I feel there was a great difference in the two, their symbols on the silver screen were more or less comparable. Seriously, we must surely admit the obvious similarity ... that neither of these sexy and beautiful women was by any standard beyond sex appeal what we can truthfully call a great actress. At the same time, each in her own particular way possessed most of the qualities Hollywood in those days found alluring and befitting the image of stardom.

Time continues to change public perception in many ways. Just as the word alluring has been almost totally lost today, so too has the true star disappeared from the Hollywood scene. Gone to the other side of the rainbow are the real stars ... Judy Garland, Joan Crawford, Bette Davis, Jean Harlow, Lana Turner (who, to me, fell into the category of Marilyn), Betty Grable (also in that category), and moving on back to Gloria Swanson, Clara Bow, Bebe Daniels, Billie Dove, and Marion Davies ... all of whom were stars of the first magnitude. All created by the studios.

Then there was Greta Garbo, greatest of them all ... the star of stars in a class by herself, along with the one and only Katharine Hepburn who, like Garbo, remains incomparable. Admittedly, Barbara Streisand matured to the degree that we must seriously consider her a contender for similar stature. Though wonderfully and gloriously unique and different from one another, these outstanding personalities have one notable quality. Character. Of course, this is the primary determining factor, which, as the old saying goes, separates the men from the boys. In this case, indeed ... the women.

And speaking of boys, we must be equally aware that there are male equivalents ... Stars of the past who were, in their own way, equally attractive and exciting. Beginning with, James Dean and Elvis Presley. Moving back in time, we remember Robert Taylor, Lawrence Olivier, Orson Welles, Doug Fairbanks, Leslie Howard and Ronald Coleman, to name but a few. Each of us can mentally create our own list of those equally qualified. But in recalling them, how do we balance the scales in the world of entertainment today? In answer, we can name good actors, of course. But where are we to find an equivalent to those who have disappeared over the horizon? Try as we will, we see that they have, except in our personal memories, become but shadow forms dimmed by light from a different sun, rising from a new direction and having a different intensity within an almost totally new world.

On another of those Friday afternoons at home, the phone rang and I recognized the voice of Jeanette the secretary saying, "Norman, there's nothing for you here right now, so please report with

Greta Garbo, the author's star or stars.

rehearsal clothes to 20th Century Fox at 9 o'clock on Monday morning. The choreographer will be Hermes Pan, and the picture is *Gentlemen Prefer Blondes*. You'll be there for three or four weeks with a possibility of remaining for another film with Vera Ellen. Whether or not you stay for the second one depends on what we have happening here. Anyway, you'll be working. We'll be in touch when you finish with Hermes. Enjoy the weekend." The phone clicked and my mind went blank.

A few days later I had a difficult time adjusting to the new environment. Whether it was Marilyn, the choreographer or the studio itself which caused this feeling I did not know then, nor have I been able to figure it out after all these years. I felt excited and intrigued at Universal, happy at Paramount, and ecstatic at MGM. Working on this particular film with Marilyn should have been a thrill, but for me it was more like a flat tire. Truthfully, I believe I was always tuned in to the loneliness and insecurity of little Norma Jean, which was almost unknown prior to her death. I never really saw the sexy and glamorous movie star she outwardly portrayed during her years of public life. Though she proved outwardly fun and delightful to be around and work with, I was unable to escape the sense of what was going on beneath that seemingly fun-loving outer shell. Others who knew her more intimately (the many biographers, in particular) are much more suited to giving a more complete picture of her famous, yet tragic life.

During those years there were four major studios doing what MGM was doing ... putting a large number of the best dancers they could find under long-term contract, something that had never been done before. Nor has it been done since. This, of course, was because we were in the thick of what's been labeled the "Era of the Great Musicals," and this was the studio's protection ... having us available whenever they wanted us.

Fox was one of the studios that had its own group, and it was only natural for them to bring dancers from other studios when some of theirs were being used on another picture. In a sense, we had simply become a commodity. They, of course, gave their own people the choice spots. Perhaps this was one of the reasons I couldn't get worked up about this number with La Monroe ... or maybe I was so in love with MGM that I was feeling a bit homesick.

When I got home at the end of our last day of work on *Gentlemen Prefer Blondes,* the casting office at MGM phoned to give me this message: "Norman there's still nothing scheduled for you here right now, so please return to 20th Century Fox tomorrow morning and report to Leonide Massine." At the sound of that name, I was glad no one in casting could see my reaction or read my thoughts. If they had, I would no doubt have ended up paying them instead of them paying me for the job I was about to begin.

The message continued: "He's remaining here in Hollywood long enough to choreograph a number for Vera Ellen in *Carnival in Costa Rica.* This will be a big Latin number and you'll no doubt be there for at least six or eight weeks. You'll probably be doing some scenes with Celeste Holm and J. Carroll Naish as well as the dance with Vera Ellen. Get a good night's rest and make sure you get there at 9 o'clock. Give me a call the day after you finish if you don't hear from me first. 'Bye ...'"

Wow! What a difference betwen my reaction to this message and the one I'd received a month ago informing me I'd be working with Marilyn. Hearing the name Leonide Massine was akin, at least in many ways, to hearing that of Vaslav Nijinsky; primarily because they had been an integral part of the great Russian Imperial Ballet, as was my first teacher, Adolph Bolm. To this day, more than fifty years later, I can still feel the excitement and emotion of hanging up the phone and saying over and over to myself: "I can't believe it... I can't believe it ... but it's true."

Marilyn Monroe, stunningly beautiful with no jewelry, just the "all American Girl" look, dressed in a Black Dress with white gloves.

This picture was taken in New York City where she was being honored for her appearance in "The Prince And The Show Girl" with Lawrence Olivier. Bill Perez was part of the welcome committee at the Italian Consulate in New York City and held a bouquet of yellow flowers to present to Marilyn Monroe.

Picture taken while living in New York City in the '60s by Bill Perez (Bijou) now living in Palm Springs, California.

Marilyn Monroe waits for her keys in her apartment elevator after attending a Ball at Madison Square Gardens in New York City in honor of the the president's birthday.

She dressed in a beautiful golden gown and white mink coat.

Picture taken on May 19, 1962 by Bill Perez (Bijou) while living in New York City in the '60s. .

Shortly before this, I'd been an usher at the Philharmonic Auditorium, the major theatre for all grand events in downtown Los Angeles, where I actually met and rubbed elbows with nearly all members of the Imperial Russian Ballet backstage. Time-wise it was the end of World War II, and certain items badly needed by stage performers were exceedingly difficult to find. One of these items, strangely enough, unless we give it serious consideration, was nothing less than a box of Kleenex ... nearly impossible to find, regardless of where one searched. This item was of course absolutely essential to all performers.

Fortunately, when I learned of this plight from the dancers, I immediately followed a hunch and contacted Roger, a friend who was manager of a Thrifty Drug Store on Hollywood Boulevard. On the morning I called him he regretfully told me what I didn't want to hear ... they were completely out of Kleenex and all other such tissues, and his particular store hadn't had any in stock for more than two weeks. That evening at the theatre I made a point of making an early appearance backstage, letting all the dancers I'd met know exactly what had happened, and at the same time assuring them my friend would make an even greater effort on their behalf. Seeing the expression on their faces I felt a deep personal sense of disappointment. Later the same evening while ushering and watching their performances from a seat in the very back row, I was determined to find a way to make them happy by the time I saw them again.

There are times, I'm sure, when each of us feels we have somehow touched the wings of an Angel. So it was that when I arrived home the same evening. I'd no more than walked through the door than I was deeply aware of something strange going on in my mind. But try as I might, I was unable to determine what it was. I looked slowly around the house, turned on different lights, then walked over to my small phonograph and placed the needle on my favorite record, *Swan Lake*. Walking slowly

Leonide Massine and Nathalie Krassovska in the film "Gaite Parisienne." Following this film, Norman was invited by Massine to sign a contract and return to London with him. Norman had to honor his contract with MGM, though, and could not take advantage of this opporutnity.

toward the sofa, I was so immediately caught up in the sounds of music that I was not quite certain of another sound, a sound that seemed to be more vibration than actual noise opposed to the music. Then it came again, louder. ... and before I picked up my phone I knew what it was, and I also knew what the strange feeling had been as I walked into the house a bit earlier.

Roger was just turning his key in the door at 7 o'clock the next morning as I crossed Hudson Avenue and entered the store behind him. While he turned on the lights he said, "Be sure to turn the lock ... I have a million things to do before we open at eight." Ten minutes later I'd paid for my purchase of gold and walked out the door....

My arrival at the Philharmonic that evening was no ordinary occasion. I had alerted the stage manager earlier in the day that I had been even more successful than I had imagined, and the reception I received upon arrival that evening was one I shall never forget. It was like a special party just for me. I was greeted as though I, too, was a member of the company and they were applauding some unusual role I'd just danced. Many hugged me. Some bowed. Nearly all had tears in their eyes ... and it showed the truth enshrined in those words, "... little things mean a lot."

The morning after receiving the more than exciting call regarding the 20th Century Fox assignment, I was up early. Not taking a chance on missing the red car at the usual time, I caught an earlier one, transferred to the Pico bus and arrived at the Fox gate just as Johnnie Ray was turning into the lot. Seeing me get off the bus, he slammed on his brakes and gave me a lift up the driveway, through the police checkpoint and into the parking lot, thus saving me the rather long walk ordinarily necessary for those who were not in the special privileges category.

Johnnie parked his car in his usual spot, at the same time suggesting we start the day with a cup of coffee before heading our separate ways. We'd met some months earlier at Ciro's and hit it off like we'd

To my Pal Norman - your buddy, Johnnie Ray

Best Norman Behave! Dan Dailey

Actors Johnnie Ray and Dan Dailey were close friends with the author.

known one another for years. It seemed natural to both of us when the evening was over and we ended up in my apartment, right there on the hill adjoining Ciro's. I'd admired Johnnie's voice and recordings since hearing him sing about the little white cloud that cried, and we learned right off the bat that we had many things in common as we continued to see one another....

That particular morning entering the coffee shop we were nearly knocked to the floor by Dan Dailey as he pushed the heavy door in our faces just as we reached for the handle.

"My God," he shouted, "look what the dog's drug in."

He laughed as Johnnie grabbed hold of his outstretched arm and pulled him back inside with us, at the same time raising his voice to match that of Dan. "Don't be so smart, Mister Dailey. Seeing you here is proof that they let anyone in ... so come on back and join us for a quick celebration. Norman begins work today with Leonide Massine, so come on and have another cup of Java with us. Even if you've had one or two or three, you can guzzle another... just to enjoy our company, if for no other reason." Dan's exaggerated facial expression was sufficient to give us an answer as the three of us found a seat and made ourselves comfortable. I kept an eye on the clock while we shot the bull. Talk included plans for our regular Saturday volleyball session at Will Rogers State Beach in Santa Monica. At this time our group was nearly as tight-knit as the famous Rat Pack, and included Peter Lawford, Van Johnson, Keenan Wynn, Bob Taylor, Monty Clift (when in town), Tom Drake, Howard Keel, John Hodiak, Robert Walker, Dan, Johnnie, and me ... just a bunch of guys with certain things in common having a great time. This was something most of us looked forward to every Saturday, with an occasional special celebration at someone's home.

Promptly at 8:55, I scooted out of the commissary, leaving Dan and Johnnie with a promise to touch base before Saturday to decide where we'd meet before heading for the beach. Rehearsals were

J. Carroll Naish was one of the stars of "Carnival in Costa Rica."

to be conducted on one of the sound stages not far away, and Massine was already warming-up off in one corner of the area where he'd be working.

I was fascinated and surprised at the casualness and lack of true technique he exhibited, feeling in my naive observation that anyone of us was capable of doing far better and showing more perfection. This was my one and only disappointment, but it was not until years later that I learned something extremely important: it is not so much what you do, but how you do it that proves a point.

Still later, this was verified over and over again in comparing the techniques of Nureyev and Barishnikof, the latter having almost flawless ability to execute, but who lacked most of the emotion and true dramatic interpretation of the former. Undoubtedly, it was similar to the greatest of all ... the brother of the lady who was responsible for my entrance into the grand and glorious professional world of dance. Perhaps if I'd had one wish during my lifetime, it would be to have personally seen Nijinsky dance. Knowing how closely he had worked with the man whose technique I was quietly and secretly criticizing, this undoubtedly was one of the primary reasons for my feeling such an honor, being right there, ready to work with him.

Suddenly, having continued to watch him from a distance as I warmed up at the barre which had been set up along one wall of the stage, my mind did a sort of flip-flop, realizing how important this very morning was ... one of those rare chances of a lifetime. I mentally examined the man more closely, knowing how very special he was ... a man who had, along with Nijinsky and Pavlova, appeared before the most illustrious audiences of Europe and those of his own country, including the Czar and Czarina. My mind swirled with recollections of page after page I'd read while researching *The Unforgettable Tragedy of Nijinsky* during my last year in college ... the book which changed my life just prior to leaving home and heading for Hollywood.

Words fail in any attempt to explain my feelings during the days and weeks that followed. Simply being with and working in the presence of this man far overshadowed the awareness of sweet and talented Vera, Celeste Holm, and J. Carroll Naish .... so much so that at times I almost forgot they were there.

When participating in the noisy whoops and hollers from the many dancers augmented by extras who had been added to the choreographed routine, I found myself joining in the fun and laughter. It reminded me of the few times I'd recently spent onstage at the Philharmonic doing similar things with the Russian Ballet ... times when they needed extras in such ballets as *Petrouchka* and I'd been one of those sent to their aid by my teacher, Adolph Bolm. Such experiences, of course, helped my own self-assurance as I began to dance with the stars, each time lessening the gap between them and me, even if only a little. And I appreciated it more and more.

On one particular day during shooting, one of my buddies and I were chatting with Vera Ellen when she came up with a special treat for us, as well as herself. "How'd you guys like to go next door and say hello to Carmen Miranda? They're filming right next to us, and maybe we'll be lucky enough to catch her on a break. It's worth a try, huh?"

Vera Ellen

To Norman, Here's wishing you oooodles of happiness always, Vera-Ellen

85

Tony, my friend, jumped at the chance with "... super idea, Vera, let's go. I've always wanted to work with her or at least meet her."

Three and-a-half minutes later, we were let through by the guard at the stage door heading toward Carmen's portable dressing room. Luck was with us as Vera approached the assistant director and whispered in his ear. She returned seconds later saying they'd been on a break for only two or three minutes.

Trailing closely behind her, we hesitated at the foot of the dressing room steps, watching hopefully as Vera knocked on the door. Then amidst the sounds made by both cast and crew surrounding us we heard a familiar voice calling out: "Come in, whoever you are." Yes, the sound of the voice was definite and unmistakable. The door opened to reveal exactly what Tony and I had anticipated ... Carmen, in full glory: from headdress down to wedgies.

The girlish shriek from both stars brought immediate attention from most of the people behind us, but was quickly shut out as Carmen grabbed Vera's arm, pulling her into the room and beckoning us to follow. Tony and I stood transfixed, watching the reactions caused by this "0-o-o-o, what a surprise visit," until we wcrc properly introduced, each receiving visible imprints of Carmen's lips on both cheeks. Worry about the imprints was the farthest thing from our minds at the moment, since we knew our faces could be retouched when we returned to our home base.

What intrigued us to the exclusion of all else was the fact that this special lady standing before us was exactly what she portrayed on the screen ... glib, vivacious, glamorous, and full of fun energy. Though outside the studio she may have truly had a flip side of this, we momentarily enjoyed watching the body language and listening to the girl talk between Carmen and Vera.

Dick Haymes, Vera Ellen, Cesar Romero, J. Carroll Naish and Celeste Holm starred in "Carnival in Costa Rica."

Ten minutes later, arriving back on our own set, I felt it would be impossible for the makeup department to wipe off the star dust which surely must have been visible on my skin as they touched up those lip-prints on my cheeks. Needless to say, the rest of the afternoon went by far more quickly than usual.

At this point my dark hair color caused by the bottle of Clairol used while filming the *Scheherezade* number at Universal was still with me. It helped to create a convincing character for this particular film, but may have even strengthened my image as Massine and his wife approached me on our last day of filming with an offer that absolutely blew me out of the water. They explained that following this film they would be returning to London to do a very lavish creation for a movie script called *The Red Shoes*. They invited me to participate in the many classical ballets Massine would be choreographing.

As they spoke, I could scarcely control my emotions, even without knowledge or forethought as to the great success the film was later to become. My mind raced ahead, already visualizing the potential of such an offer, but I could only thank them and explain my situation relating to MGM. I let them know, too, that I would do everything I could to cancel my contract ... even though I was fully aware that this offer was for only one film; as opposed to the security of seven years ... and that it would take place thousands of miles from here.

The next day, after a near sleepless night, I made a special trip to the studio to explain what had taken place, and asked for a leave of absence. The request was denied. Had I known then what I would later realize after viewing *The Red Shoes* I may well have gone so far as to tear up my contract.

Had I done the right thing when I made the decision to go on dancing with the stars? Or had I missed the greatest chance of my life?

CHAPTER EIGHT

The Pirate

Vincente Minnelli, Judy Garland's husband during these years, was definitely one of my favorite directors. Not only because he directed many of the musicals in which I worked, but because he was extremely creative and sensitive in all of his film work. He was a true individual and his efforts proved it. Perhaps more than any other source it was he who contributed most in my own total awareness of the movie business. Because of my admiration for all he stood for in the giant MGM arena I found myself being immersed in many facets of the industry besides dancing. Though he had no way of knowing it, Judy's husband was without a doubt a strong and major influence in my creative life.

In looking back at mentor-like figures, some may wonder about the one and only Cecil B. De Mille, whom I was fortunate enough to work for during a couple of loan-outs to Paramount Pictures. In comparison, I would admit to it only on one level: his overall reputation as a truly great director. Certainly, that fact is indisputable. But from my viewpoint, it stops there. True enough,

Scenes from "The Pirate" starring Gene Kelly and Judy Garland, 1948

there was only one De Mille ... and one was enough! Tyrant, dictator, bully and an egotistical genius. But who needs to work with or for such a character when there exists an individual who is thoughtful, polite, considerate, and creative? Vincente Minnelli was just such a man. While one was ruling his slaves at Paramount the other was creatively working with his Metro Goldwyn Mayer family.

In the realm of musicals during the '40s I am yet uncertain why I (regardless of dear Judy) found no special thrill working in the two dance numbers with both Gene Kelly and Judy in *The Pirate*. Nor does it seem sufficient to say it was merely that I had become quickly spoiled by the flash and glamour of beautiful people, both female and male, along with jazzy music, with feathers, sequins, and tremendous large sets, all of which were an integral part of it. Whatever my feelings, or lack of them, I acknowledge that *The Pirate* viewed today as a fantasy-parody of old-time movie swashbucklers, was far ahead of its time in the annals of movie-making. Minnelli's imagination, blending magnificently with the choreography of Robert Alton (the man responsible for my contract) to create numbers both lavish and colorful were tremendous additions to one of the cleverest Cole Porter scores ever to hit the screen. Regardless of all else, working day-after-day, week-after-week again with our Judy was certainly more than enough to offset any personal opinions of mine relating to whatever I felt lacking. As a matter of fact, it was this film, which proved to be a transition period for Judy, from innocence to sophistication, both in song and as a full-fledged comedian. In other words, all of us saw her suddenly fully mature. Grown up. Too, it was a time in which those of us who saw her on a day-to-day, week-to-week, month-to-month basis became very aware of an increasing dependency upon pills.

In the beginning, we were aware that it was only a matter of taking one to wake up ... a natural assumption because of overwork. Before long, it was one to get through the long strenuous day. And finally, another to allow sleep at night. This increasing need seemed slowly and casually an extension of a commonly-understood answer to a simple need caused by what seemed perfectly logical: sheer exhaustion due to pressure put upon a strong, yet frail individual who was being pushed more and more, one role upon another, with little or no rest. .. all of which could, we felt, have been avoided through nothing more or less than an extended care-free vacation, away from all that fame and fortune could not supply. Oh, yes, Judy was given a day here, a day there. No one will deny that. But never enough to pull together the mind, body, and spirit of one so creatively gifted ... one so small, so frail as the real Judy. In the eyes of Studio Moguls, she was their Giantess! Unfortunately, like the rest of us. Judy Garland was also human.

Hatfield, pictured above, right, in a movie trailer for "The Picture of Dorian Gray" and above, left, in a scene from the film.

The cast included Hurd Hatfield (Dorian Gray); Donna Reed (Gladys Hallward); Angela Lansbury (Sibyl Vane); and Peter Lawford (David Stone) among others. The film won an Academy Award in 1945 for best cinematography in black and white, Harry Stradling.

CHAPTER NINE

Dorian Gray Comes to Life

Van Johnson was without a doubt one of the biggest and most popular stars ever turned out by MGM. He was also one of the nicest guys I've ever known, and was definitely one of those few big stars who was able to keep both feet on the ground. He also had a way of making you feel like the most important person in the world when you spoke to him.

James Dean, whom I cared about very much, was oblivious to the moods and preferences of others for the most part. There were times, though, when he gave people all he had. He was far from being an extrovert, which was so much a part of Van's personality. Jimmy had natural charisma and total animal magnetism.

For those who recall Hurd Hatfield's performance in *The Picture of Dorian Gray*, they'll remember his was a different sort of magnetism; different, but subtly inviting. This was no doubt what attracted me to him in the beginning. I liked him even though I was far from pleased that he was given the starring role in the film for which I, too, had tested. I'd wanted that part more than anything in the world at that particular time and was none to pleasant about losing it to him. The truth, when Angela Lansbury, who had a small but wonderful part in the picture, introduced us I was definitely not my usual charming self.

Positive magnetism often overcomes negative emotion and I found myself more attracted to Hurd than I cared to admit. The jealousy and anger I felt at losing the part began to dwindle each time he left the set where he was working and walked across to stand at the rehearsal hall door where I was working. He pretended to be interested in the whole group as we rehearsed, but he was really watching me.

At the end of the first week following our introduction, he invited me to spend the weekend with him in Ojai. When I accepted his invitation, I realized I was no longer irritated by him getting "my" part in the movie. Meanwhile, the pavement between Stage 10 where Hurd was shooting, and Rehearsal Hall A where I continued rehearsals, was well traveled by one or the other of us during every possible break.

If I recall correctly, we were working on a number called "Mack The Black" for *The Pirate*, starring Gene Kelly and Judy. It seemed like a coincidence when Judy whispered in my ear; "It seems your secret admirer isn't being so secretive these last few days. I hope you guys enjoy your weekend." This happened on the Friday afternoon Hurd and I were planning our first get-together in Ojai. Before I could reply, Kelly whisked her away.

I'd never been to the small art colony of Ojai prior to this trip, and time has only slightly diminished my memories of that weekend. He picked me up at home early that Friday evening and delivered me

"Hurd Hatfield and I were so close, no thought was given to having this photo autographed."

to my door forty-eight hours later. All that happened during those two days and nights helped to form deep feelings between us. Those memories are definitely a part of my magical storehouse of MGM memories.

The first evening was wonderfully fun, relaxed, and not without humor. We dined in a quaint restaurant, then browsed in a few small shops and art galleries before going to the movies. We ended up in a tiny Ice Cream Parlor after the movie. Afterward, we drove to the home of one of Hurd's friends who'd been kind enough to invite us for this first get together. Though anxious to excuse ourselves and call it a day, we spent an hour or so in the beautiful living room sipping strong European coffee and visiting with his friend. At last we bid adieu and headed for separate bedrooms. (I forgot to mention that this friend was a sweet and kind woman who'd been sort of a mother figure to Hurd for some time. She obviously knew about his relationships with certain individuals who sometimes visited her home with him as well.)

I was surprised at the separate bedrooms. I'll admit to being somewhat frustrated when Hurd walked me down a long hallway and politely showed me to my room. He gave no explanation and made no apologies as he opened the door, backed away and nodded as he said good-night.

Less than thirty minutes later, lying in bed alone, I heard a sound from a curtained area above and to the right of the bed. Looking up I was amazed to see the curtain move slowly to one side and Hurd's head poking through. I suddenly realized the curtains hid a window that was large enough to crawl through.

Putting his fingers to his lips and whispering, he told me to come on in. No further invitation was necessary. In less time than it took to say "abracadabra," I was through the window and lying beside him in his bed. (In this day and age we thoroughly understand, at least in part, what occurs when two guys of like-mind with no coercion hit the sack together. Therefore, no elaboration is necessary to tell you most of what occurred until shortly before sunrise.)

At one point during these hours, Hurd quietly and rather mysteriously whispered to me, "Do you have any idea who the last guy was who crawled through that window?" By this time being I was exhausted and sleepy, and could only move my head back and forth against his shoulder in negative response. Holding me even closer, he again whispered, "Monty Clift ... but right now I'm really glad you're here." And because I, too, liked Monty very much, the two of us fell fast asleep sharing a similar dream.

To Norman
Hedy Lamarr
1945

This photo is "far from being the lady I knew when she turned me into a frog," Norman said.

CHAPTER TEN

Hedy LaMarr and the Frog

When the phone rang around 4 p.m. one Friday afternoon, I instinctively knew it was the studio calling. *Is this going to be another of those fill-in jobs, or will it be a chance to really dance again?* I wondered. I picked up a coin from the table, flipped it, then answered after the third ring.

My first hunch had been correct. It was the studio, and the first words I heard were disappointing. "Norman, please report at nine o'clock Monday morning for some sort of a work interview. Come directly to casting and perhaps I'll be able to tell you more than I can right now. The only thing I know at the moment is that you'll be doing something with Hedy LaMarr. You don't need to wear anything special, so just come as you are. Have a nice weekend, and we'll see you Monday." There was no further conversation. The call left me with sort of a blank feeling.

The only good thing I could imagine coming from this was meeting Hedy LaMarr. For me this was a definite plus. The thought of meeting her colored my entire weekend which included a wonderful evening of stars and music at the Hollywood Bowl, followed by a different but equally enjoyable time at my favorite Hollywood Boulevard hangout.

I made it a habit never to imbibe on Sunday evenings, so on Monday morning I showed up fresh and alert at casting. I was eager to learn how I'd be connected with the gorgeous Ms. LaMarr.

My instructions were brief, simple, and vague. "Sorry I can't give you any information," Jeanette said. "Just walk over to Wardrobe and tell them we sent you. You'll be directed from there."

Not sensing any sort of urgency, I stopped at the commissary for a cup of coffee and found myself immediately joined by Van Johnson and Keenan Wynn. We'd no more than started our little bull session than we spotted Tom Drake walking through the door. The four of us took a table and spent a good half hour catching up on studio and Hollywood gossip. (At this time, the public was mostly unaware of the private lives of Keenan and Van, who were at the height of stardom. Their private lives were successfully hidden to protect their macho screen images as well as the general public's opinion of them.) I found out that both of them had recently been forbidden to ride motorcycles for the duration of their contracts to the studio due to a serious accident that could easily have ended Van's life.

Tom had an image of the boy next door and was teamed up with June Allyson in a film by the same name. After that he worked with canine star Lassie in the macho war movie, *Hold High the Torch*. This movie seemed to rub off on his personal life and he, though primarily remaining closeted, began to take on a lifestyle most insiders felt was more fitting to his true personality and character.

As the four of us headed out the door, Van made the remark that it had been a great chat and there was no reason why we couldn't make it happen more often. Keenan agreed, tossing in his remark that "If we can't ride anymore, the least we can do is keep getting together and catch up on what's going on .... so let's do it, gentlemen. Let's do it." He let the heavy door close behind as we went our separate ways.

At wardrobe, I was instructed to walk over to the prop department and get measured. That's all they knew. Five minutes later, I was being measured so they could turn me into a frog ... but not before I proved myself capable of jumping a sufficient distance from a crouched position. With this information my thoughts about having signed on as a contract dancer took a nosedive of considerable depth until the two magic words did a replay in my head and I calmed down a bit. Yes, I would gladly do it for Hedy LaMarr. Perhaps if all went well I might even be willing to croak a bit ... if the script called for it.

Three days later there was a second frog fitting. This time the body, which was made from something resembling rubber, had been finished enough that I was able to climb into it and tell them how it felt. It had to be flexible enough that I could move around easily. After another two days, I found myself crawling into something that resembled a giant spray-painted frog, complete with warts, thick rough skin and huge, bulging, glassy eyes. Director Thorpe gave his approval. By this time he was fully convinced that my legs were good for more than what I had originally been contracted to do ... dance.

I learned that the movie was titled *Her Highness and the Bellboy*, and when shooting began one week later it was uncomfortable fun. With no actual rehearsal, I was given detailed instructions for what I was to do. The setting for "Froggie" was the windowsill of a beautiful boudoir where Hedy lay sleeping in her luxurious bed, dreaming of her very own Prince Charming. In the dream she sees this huge frog (me) perched on her windowsill, staring down at her. Inside the frog head I butted my head against the throat of the costume, and with some sound effects added later in the dubbing room, she imagined the prince was communicating with her.

Awakening from the dream, she sees that "Froggie" is real. In a very ladylike way she rises, sits on the edge of the bed and slowly and deliberately puts on a filmy lace negligee. She moves closer and closer to the window, all the time keeping her eyes locked on her frog prince. At this point my instructions were to lean forward and hop down (ugh!) from the ledge, landing on the soft carpet almost at her feet. Then I was to raise my head, which was not exactly easy, and stare into her beautiful eyes. Absolutely mesmerized with what she found herself doing, she leaned forward and kissed me. (Alas, I felt nothing through the frog head, and later had no imprint of lipstick to prove what took place.)

Just like the fairy tale, when she kissed her frog, he (I) slowly rose up, becoming taller and taller, closer and closer, until the director called, "Cut!" At that exact moment, I (the frog) somehow, with help from a member of the prop shop, managed to disappear to make way for Prince Charming (Robert Walker). He stood in exactly the space I'd just vacated. At "Roll 'em!" from director Thorpe, our prince looked upward into the beautiful face of his love from a squatting position. Then just as Froggie had done, he rose slowly until Hedy kissed his lips the same way she had kissed Froggie. He got to experience his kiss, though.

I already had a connection to the film's leading man. Shortly after my arrival at MGM, I'd met Robert through a mutual friend and learned we'd both been born in Salt Lake City. We had a special bond during the few remaining years before his death. At his funeral back in Utah, his mother read a poem I'd written and mailed to her for his memorial service. I'd always felt he was special and have never forgotten him.

Robert Walker, pictured on the right in "The Clock" which also starred Judy Garland and was directed by Arthur Freed, portrayed Prince Charming in "Her Highness and the Bellboy."

To Norman
With fond Regards
Sincerely
Frank Sinatra

Small photo shows the author as he appeared in the film, "Anchors Aweigh," with Frank Sinatra.

CHAPTER ELEVEN

Frankie

Simply being in the business does not guarantee you'll become a star, but some people possess qualities that predispose them to stardom. During the making of his second movie, Frank Sinatra exhibited them all. Those of us working with him at MGM in the early '40s wondered just how famous he would become.

I hadn't started to collect photos and autographs from the stars at the studio at this point, much to my regret now, but I sensed that Frankie was so special I approached him for an autograph. He was not too well known at this point, and was probably flattered by my request.

My clearest memory of Frankie was his pleasant smile and gentle manner. He was so friendly and easy going, everyone felt comfortable approaching him. His personality was similar to that of the ever-gracious and popular star, Van Johnson.

When we were filming *Anchors Aweigh*, which starred Frankie and Gene Kelly, some of the contract dancers also worked as extras since there were no big production numbers going on at the moment. They called us "glorified extras" probably to boost our morale during the many jobs we performed other than dancing. We often joked amongst ourselves about it, saying things like, "Oh, well, what the hell! A dollar is a dollar, so no use to holler." Corny, yes, but were were still grateful for the work, since many of our friends were unemployed at the moment.

As suggested by the title, this movie was a film about the Navy. The sequence we worked in was a locker-room scene. We had no idea whether it was located on land or on a ship, since we were never given a script. We just did what we were told to do by the first assistant. We were in true Navy garb, and for a week or more during dialogue and close-ups between Gene and Frankie we were involved primarily in doing nothing more than quietly joking among ourselves during the process of taking-off and putting-on our clothes over and over again until the stars had remembered their lines to the director's satisfaction. Basically, we were the "eye candy" for this particular scene.

One of the other things I remember fondly about Frankie was his generosity. Whether it was genuine or not is not for me to say, but my impression was that it was real. I recall when, at the end of filming on this particular picture during a huge celebration on the set, he presented beautiful gold watches to all of the special people involved with making the film a success. This included the director, assistant director, co-stars, cameraman and head electrician, as well as the choreographer. Though such special occasions, including the giving of expensive gifts, were not all that unusual in those days, it is something which has stuck in my memory. There was something very genuine and meaningful in the way Frankie presented the gifts and the words he spoke while handing them to each individual. To him, this wasn't just another gift, it was something to be remembered. Even today, I know all of those who received these gifts knew they were special.

That was the Sinatra I knew, the young man who took the time when autographing a photo for me, to say just a bit more. Those little things, as the old song says, meant a lot.

Ziegfeld Follies

CHAPTER TWELVE

Ziegfeld Follies

Salaries ... then and now. Two favorite oldies (*Pennies From Heaven* and *We're in the Money*) run musically through my mind to explain what I mean. In 1943, MGM contract dancers began a new and exciting career at a salary considerably higher than we'd ever had before. Furthermore, neither MGM nor any other Hollywood movie studio had previously made an offer to put anyone other than movie stars under contract for as long as seven years. It was unheard of.

But things immediately following the Busby Berkeley era brought forth new ideas and new thinking. The law of supply and demand also created re-evaluation of our weekly salaries and the length of our contracts. We were the envy of every dancer in Hollywood. Our incomes had jumped from an ordinary $68.75 per week to $100, with a pay guarantee of 48 weeks per year, whether we worked or not. It was a dream come true!

Fred Astaire and Lucille Bremer in Ziegfeld Follies.

When I say we, I mean the elite 27 girls and 27 boys who auditioned and were selected from all the dancers in both Hollywood and New York. We all felt extremely lucky, acknowledged, and special. I was one of these individuals, but I had no idea just how fortunate and extra special I would soon become.

Rehearsals had just begun on the "Limehouse Blues" number for the film, *Ziegfeld Follies*, starring Fred Astaire, and introducing Lucille Bremer. It was no secret around the studio that Lucille, a pretty chorus girl, had recently been brought from Broadway by our producer, Arthur Freed, and was at this moment his private property who could do no wrong. She would soon be given a starring role in *Yolanda and the Thief*. As a partner to Astaire in both *Ziegfeld* and *Yolanda*, Lucille provided an interesting change of pace for Fred after being partners with Eleanor Powell and Ginger Rogers.

Ziegfeld Follies

Recently, a potential new star had been discovered and brought through the same iron gates to join the MGM family. Though an unknown, she was talented, slim, graceful, gorgeous and had amazingly long, beautiful legs. I immediately recognized her as a ballet classmate I'd danced with many times in rehearsals at the Nico Charisse Studio in Hollywood. I was delighted to learn she'd be dancing in our "Limehouse Blues" number, with David Lober, a close friend of mine, as her partner. Choreographer Robert Alton, who was familiar with both dancers, had selected the two.

At this moment, fate stepped in and whisked David off to appear in a Broadway show, leaving Alton high and dry and looking for a suitable dancer for a dream sequence with the new potential star on the MGM horizon. This latest catastrophe had happened on a Friday afternoon.

As I walked through the gate later that day, thinking of our weekly Santa Monica State Beach volleyball agenda, I was stopped by the guard with a message to report to Rehearsal Hall B tomorrow morning at ten with rehearsal clothes. The only redeeming thing about this was double pay on my next paycheck. Later that evening I phoned both Johnnie Ray and Dan Dailey to let them know I might not be able to join them until late in the morning for the end of the game at the earliest, and might not make it until time for brunch at our favorite hangout across the highway from Will Rogers State Beach. Both guys insisted I make it, no matter how late it was.

The next morning at 10 sharp four of us converged on the floor of Rehearsal Hall B at exactly the same moment: Robert Alton, choreographer; Roger Edens, piano accompanist; myself; and Cyd Charisse. She'd come to MGM shortly after me, and what was about to get noticed in a big way.

On this particular morning, I learned that my friend, David Lober, had unknowingly done me a tremendous favor when he suddenly decided a lead dance spot in New York was preferable to being partners with the unknown Cyd Charisse in her first movie musical assignment. Bob Alton was aware that I was taking classes and working with Cyd in regular dance instruction with both Nico Charisse and Nijinska. If he hadn't known this, he might well have looked outside MGM to replace David. It was truly fortunate for all of us that the episode turned out as it did. Both Cyd and I felt comfortable as Alton put us through what seemed like a thousand and one technical combinations to the accompaniment of suitable piano music provided by Roger Edens.

Though we felt we'd immediately sold Bob on the idea that he'd made a good choice pairing us, he seemed eager to convince himself we were truly capable of performing all of the strange and wonderful movements he had in mind for this extravaganza. After approximately 45 minutes of grueling workout, Alton announced his decision. I was to be David Lober's replacement and partner to Cyd in the haunting and mystical dream sequence.

At the same time, I would be acting as dance-in for Astaire. Alton's decision to use me as Astaire's dance-in caused more than a little jealousy among some of my fellow contract dancers, particularly those he'd brought from Broadway when MGM lured him away from New York. Things didn't get any better when word got out about my salary hike either.

This meant I would learn Fred's part, along with Cyd and all of the dancers involved in the overall number. I would also be teaching it to him from time to time since his shooting schedule caused him to be away at another stage. The entire concept was all new to me. As I walked to wardrobe for my first fitting, my mind was a jumble of questions without answers. At the moment I felt only a need to focus my mind on making sure the fantasy-like costume, already nearly completed for David, would fit me.

By this time it was past 11 o'clock and I knew my buddies were well into the volleyball game, and would no doubt assume I was unable to join them. Once I'd left the wardrobe department and headed

Norman was featured with Cyd Charisse in "Ziegfeld Follies," which was her first film.

The author was having fun with this fantasy bird costume that was to be used in the film "Ziegfeld Follies." The costumes for the film were designed by Irene Sharaff of New York City. The original sketch is pictured above.

out the gate, I looked up at Leo with a silent cry for help. My answer came as if by magic. Turning left and walking quickly toward Washington Boulevard, I was startled by a loud honk from an auto approaching from behind me. Surprise of surprises, it was none other than my pal, Johnnie Ray.

Pulling alongside me, he leaned across the seat and threw open the door. Not waiting for questions or answers, I jumped in beside him and pulled the door shut as he gunned the motor and took off. We were less than 500 feet from Washington Boulevard, so neither of us spoke until Johnny had checked for traffic and turned left, barely making the green light. I let out a sigh of relief, knowing exactly what had happened and where we were headed ... Santa Monica Beach.

Alton knew that once he'd set the complete routine with me it would be no problem for Fred to pick it up in a few rehearsals. Meanwhile, Bob and I spent many weeks choreographing the number with more than 50 dancers before Fred arrived to watch me go through his part. I would go through it phrase by phrase, movement by movement until he felt comfortable with it and finally took over the role.

"Limehouse Blues" was a dramatic number set to the old tune by the same name. It was for this very reason Bob had selected me to replace David, because he knew I was capable of projecting an enormous amount of drama and feeling into the number. Astaire, with his own unique lighter style, naturally saw it somewhat differently. His interpretation bothered me as I watched him make changes. However, it was his number to do with as he liked and there was nothing I could say or do.

It was 1944, and within six months, I had gone from $100 a week to $500 a week as dance-in for Astaire. While dancing with Cyd my pay jumped to $1,000! All of this was overwhelming to a kid who had hitchhiked his way to Hollywood on a truck from a small town in Idaho just four years earlier.

Aside from this I must admit something else. The biggest lift to my ego was when I walked into the rehearsal hall the following Monday morning and found a special director's chair with NORMAN spelled out in big black letters exactly like the one next to it which read: CYD CHARISSE. It verified my own personal belief that what you dream about comes about.

The dance Alton created for Cyd and me, literally a number within a number, was pure fantasy. The two of us were portraying two giant birds in a dreamlike and mystical oriental cock-fight minus the fighting. The acclaimed New York costume and set designer, Irene Sharaff, was brought to the studio to create the sets and costumes for our number. We learned there was no end to her creative imagination. Everything was dramatically unreal and seemed to take place in another world.

Cyd and I were dressed in solid blue. My costume had a six-foot tail of hand-dyed shaded chicken feathers. The dancers working with us were costumed with equal imagination to appear as though they were part of a forest which surrounded us everywhere we moved. It was a *Wizard Of Oz*-type wonderland.

As suggested by the name "Limehouse Blues", Fred and Lucille were a Chinese couple walking along a dimly lit street surrounded by exotic and alluring shops. At one point Lucille stops, leans down and admires a beautiful fan, fully open and surrounded by many other intriguing articles displayed behind the window. Shortly thereafter, Fred breaks the window, reaches through the opening and slowly picks up the fan, admiring it as he draws it to him … only to be shot by someone from behind. As he falls to the cobblestone street, he looks sadly at the fan, his vision blurs and he collapses against the base of the window amidst broken glass.

The camera then creates what he visualizes as he dies. After a fade-out followed by an equally fantasy-like fade-in, Cyd and I appear in our own dramatic scene.

The number Alton choreographed for us took three months to rehearse and more than three months to film on Stage 30, the largest sound stage on the lot. This was the same stage where the Esther Williams swimming extravaganzas took place.

One day during the shooting of our number, both cast and crew were shocked to see Arthur Freed, our producer, walk in and sit down with none other than Louella Parsons, the most feared, bigger than life Hollywood newspaper columnist. Here was the most powerful woman in the industry, even though she wasn't a part of it, and she was here to see our number. She could make or break stars overnight. These thoughts drifted through my mind as she sat watching Cyd and me dance. At one point during a break, Mr. Freed called us over and introduced us. I've never forgotten the words that came from her lips as she turned to our producer and said, "Arthur, this can very well be your next dance team."

Cyd and I danced through the next shot with no retake; we were on top of the world after that compliment. If Queen Louella had this idea, then surely it would happen. Fortunately for Cyd, the star of MGM who had even more power than Louella (Fred Astaire, himself), was standing within earshot. The dye had been cast and he would take Cyd as his partner for his next film.

The following Saturday, *Life* magazine came to MGM to shoot photos which would make history. On a specially-constructed tiered, grandstand-type platform just inside the great doors on the side of Stage 30, the soon-to-be-famous photos would show every major star of the world's largest and most prestigious motion picture studio, along with a few potential stars-in-the-making. And in front-row-center, the photo would show none other than dear Lassie ... a Star among Stars.

Yes, the entire studio of stars was not only invited, but required to appear for this shoot, including Cyd, the newest kid-on-the-block. But not Norman. Mr. Fred Astaire had taken care of that. I, being

Lucille Bremer wrote the following: To Norman, The only bubble dancing rooster I know." in reference to his costume for "Ziegfeld Follies" which was never seen by the movie-going public.

still wet behind the ears, was somewhat surprised but not particularly bothered as I happily joined my buddies at the beach for a wonderful day of fun and freedom.

Monday morning. Reality hit when I stopped at the commissary and spotted Lucille Bremer, who was about to leave. After giving her a brief report on my great Saturday with the guys, most of whom she knew, I asked how it went at the session with *Life*. I also asked her just why I'd been lucky enough not to be included. She suddenly got a strange expression on her face. She looked me straight in the eyes, opened her mouth as though to speak, but nothing came out.

Still not getting the message, I looked back at her and asked, "What is it, Lucille? Is something wrong?"

She hesitated, but only for a moment before blurting out, "Oh, Norman, didn't you hear? Don't you know? Your whole number with Cyd has been cut, and ..." She couldn't finish the sentence or contain her tears as she took me in her arms for one long moment, then suddenly let me go and rushed out through the commissary door.

By this time, I was no longer in a mood for coffee. I followed Lucille out the door, then turned and walked directly to the main cutting room. I needed to hear the truth from the only person whose story I could believe, Al Akst, head cutter for this department. In a matter of seconds after entering the building, I was standing face to face asking a question, at the same time fearing what I now heard. Al's answer was direct. Simple. "I'm sorry to say this, Norman, but you have to know the truth." He hesitated before going on. "The number was great. You and Cyd did it and made it work. Seeing it for the first time, we were excited about it. Even Freed, who kept saying something like 'Louella was right. These two can be my next team.'

"Then Fred was called in to look at it. There was a lot of discussion between Arthur and Fred before Fred won out ..." At this point he made a gesture with his finger across his throat before completing his sentence. "He kept insisting the dream sequence with you and Cyd made the number too long." As I turned toward the door, Al touched me on the shoulder adding, "I'm really sorry, Norman. It was one helluva number. You and Cyd, that's the kind of thing I hate to see end up on the cutting room floor."

Yes, one helluva number, and I'm glad I was not the first and only one to say it. Further more, other than the beauty and glamour of the number itself being wasted, it meant the loss of hundreds of thousands of dollars, months of rehearsals, weeks of shooting ... and a dream gone up in smoke. I later learned that other entire numbers were also cut from the film, numbers starring such big time stars as Fanny Bryce, James Melton and Jimmy Durante. At least I was in good company there on the cutting room floor.

CHAPTER THIRTEEN

Detour From Dancing

On this particular Monday morning, attired in my best pair of shorts, sweat sox, running shoes plus an appropriate T-shirt, I left Leo the Lion roaring at the gate and headed for Stage 15 as I'd been instructed to do on the previous Friday. Moments later, I was greeted by two other contract dancers who'd arrived a little early. They knew exactly as much information about the interview as I did ... nothing. Just then, a limo arrived and we were greeted by Al Jennings, an assistant director who usually worked with Richard Thorpe, well-known director of all Lassie films. He asked us to just take it easy until everyone arrived.

It was obvious that Stage 15 was not being used, so we were still in the dark as far as what we'd be doing. A few carpenters and stagehands were busy inside working on some sort of outdoor scenery that was just beginning to take shape. Again, no clue as to what was going on for us.

We helped ourselves to some coffee and sauntered back outside for a doughnut from the catering wagon. From the relaxed mood of the workers, it was easy to tell that nothing would be happening on this particular stage for at least a few days. The mood and tempo of all those around us was much too casual and laid-back to give any indication of what was in store for us.

Thirty minutes later we learned who we'd been waiting for. Finally, Richard Thorpe emerged from a studio limo along with three others, one from wardrobe, one from the prop shop and the other from the script department. Al Jennings motioned the three of us to follow as they headed for a large corner of the stage away from the area occupied by the workers. As he began reading off our names, four other contract dancers who'd originally been sent to the wrong location joined us. Seconds later all eyes were focused on a tall, well-built man who sprinting through the open door and halted in the middle of our group. He panted, "Sorry to be late. We had to finish lining up the last shot before they could let me go."

Thorpe, glanced up at him and said his timing was perfect. The sprinter, attired in a snug-fitting white track-suit with a large number 19 on it walked directly in front of me, and I noticed that Mr. Thorpe's secretary wasn't shy about checking him out from head to toe. No one blamed her, since he was perfectly put together, including the short tousled blonde hair which topped it all off.

Al said they were looking for someone whose legs most closely matched up with the track-suited Adonis. The guy from the script department explained that in the story there was a comedy situation where this guy was being chased while running a marathon through a wooded area. "At one point," he said, "he spies an abandoned sewer pipe approximately 10 feet long, just barely big enough around for him to crawl into and hide. So that's exactly what he does ... dives into it just far enough not to be visible to the guy chasing him. His pursuer naturally runs past him and continues on up the trail, unaware that he's lost his prey. Then our hero, no longer worried about his enemy, finds he has a serious problem. He backs up a few inches, wiggles his big feet and attempts to reverse himself and get out the same way he got in. But, he's stuck - really stuck! He wiggles, squirms, moans and groans and finally manages to back up far enough so his feet, ankles, and calves are showing."

The guy from the script department smiles at our hero, watching his reaction, then continues, "According to the script our runner, stuck in the pipe and realizing he'll never make it out backwards, renews his moaning, groaning, stretching, and clawing and makes his way toward the far end of the pipe. The camera is now pointing toward his head and we're able to see him struggling." Thorpe interrupted, saying, "We won't divulge the rest of the story just now except to say that our hero finally makes it out alive. Actually, he emerges just far enough to raise his head and look back over his shoulder, and this is where we see a view of his feet, ankles, and hairy blond legs at the far end of the pipe."

All of us finally realized why we were there as Thorpe concluded his explanation. "At this point no dialogue is necessary. The look on our hero's face tells it all. He has stretched himself at least four feet and now realizes just how serious his problem is. That, my dear young fellows, is why you are here this morning. We need to see which one of you is walking around with a pair of legs that match his."

At this point, the sprinter was standing a mere three paces from me, looking all of us up and down. It was difficult to keep a straight face as all the decision-maker's eyes wandered slowly from our crotches to our feet. They stopped from time to time to whisper some brief remark to one another. The real coup-de-grace came when Al stepped forward and barked: "Okay fellas, will all of you turn slowly to the right? We need to get a look at the calves of your legs." We turned, stood still and waited.

Suddenly, it was over. Al's voice belted out what seemed more an apology that an announcement, "That's all, fellas. Sorry to have kept you so long. Norman, please step over here. The rest of you are dismissed."

I followed the order, and the man I was to provide legs for walked up and introduced himself, adding, "Well partner, this might even end up being fun whenever we get to it." His genuine manner and smile made me feel good. He wasn't a star, only a glorified bit-player with dreams of stardom. He looked like he might have what it took to become a star from what I could see. As he turned to walk away he looked back over his shoulder and added, "Hey, Buddy, we got at least one thing in common ... good legs" Then he was gone and I didn't see him again until we shot the scene several days later.

It was fun when we got to it. What's strange is I don't remember his name or the name of the film now. In those days I was never a fan of the films I worked in, large or small. I just enjoyed being a part of all that went on. Personally, everything was important in those days ... even a guy looking back from a sewer-pipe at his (my) legs and feet farther away than any human being could ever stretch. It was things like this that made the difference in work, even during those times when I was not exactly dancing with the stars.

CHAPTER FOURTEEN

Waterlogged with Esther Williams

Esther Williams is a name that brings back special memories, primarily because I felt I'd never have the opportunity to work in one of her films because I wasn't a good swimmer. I could dog-paddle around a pool, but never in a million years could I convince anyone of my ability to participate with those swimmers who appeared in the sort of scenes I'd watch in movies starring Esther.

Thus, my next call from the casting office took me by complete surprise. I was asked to report to Stage 30 for a three-day swimming scene with the one and only Esther. When I tried to explain my limited swimming ability the voice on the other end of the phone refused to take me seriously. "Never mind, you won't be featured, Norman, you'll just be in the pool or maybe sitting around sunning yourself. Just show up with a nice pair of trunks. Oh, and don't forget, no red or white. Good-bye."

Still in a state of surprise and elation, I hung up and began an immediate search for something suitable to wear. No red and no white. I was still wondering whether this was because it would get too much attention if it caused problems with lighting. Laughing to myself, I wondered if maybe Esther's costume was primarily red and white. I certainly didn't want to take attention away from her, so I settled on a pair of vivid blue trunks. I figured wearing this pair will at least get me noticed, but not quite enough to stop the show or steal the scene.

(As an aside, let me jump ahead to a scene many months later, which took place in my home-town of Buhl, Idaho, at the one theatre in town. The film in which I was about to participate was being shown there and my own mother and father as well as my seven-year-old sister were there to watch. Apparently, the vivid blue swimming trunks, though not exactly electric, caught the attention of Doris Lee even before my parents caught sight of me dog paddling. Yes, it was the very first time any of them had seen me on screen, and as Dad reported in a letter the following week, "When you swam to the edge of the pool and got out, Doris Lee spotted you right away. She stood straight up from her seat and yelled, 'Look! There's Norman!' Everyone in the theatre turned and laughed. Of course most of them know you, so afterwards we were almost mobbed in the lobby." Such is life in small town, Idaho.)

The next morning found me exiting from the big red car on Venice Boulevard as usual. Five minutes later, I entered the studio at the Washington Street Gate rather than main gate. It was another of those mornings when I arrived nearly half an hour early and immediately headed for the coffee shop to hobnob with some of my friends who were there as extras on other pictures.

I was in makeup longer than usual on this day, since all I'd be wearing was a pair of swim-trunks and my body was not dark enough. This taught me a good lesson and from then until I left the studio

Norman's first experience on an Esther Williams film was quite revealing.

To Norman —
all the luck in
the world to a
fellow actor!
Sincerely,
Esther Williams

years later, I saw to it that I spent nearly every weekend either at the beach or in my backyard sans everything except the briefest trunks to keep my tan.

Once inside Stage 30, clad in a light cotton robe which contrasted nicely with the blue swim trunks I had brought from home and thong sandals supplied by wardrobe, I found myself surrounded by a large number of swimmers and sunbathers. Many of them were under contract like me and I recognized several of them. Esther and her co-star, Van Johnson, hadn't arrived on the set yet, so most of us relaxed around the pool or strolled around, coffee in one hand and doughnut in the other, exchanging tidbits of gossip. The stage was comfortably cool, but heated up considerably when the giant klieg lights were turned on.

This stage was completely different from all the others on the MGM lot. This one was gigantic. This particular set had immense areas covered with removable wooden floors, rather than solid cement. Why? This was the stage where the swimming scenes for all of Esther Williams' films took place. There was also space underground, completely surrounding the pool, which contained rooms with glass walls facing the pool so the cameras could shoot underwater sequences.

After the stars arrived, the entire morning was spent in the pool while lights and cameras were adjusted to cover the scene. During all preliminaries, of course, Esther and Van were elsewhere while stand-ins took their place patiently working along with the rest of us until technicalities had been worked out and the director was ready for a preliminary run-through of the scene prior to the first actual shot.

The first scene was simple, and took far less time than the technical work, which had taken more than two hours. Shooting finally began for a dialogue between Esther and Van who were seated at a table beside the pool where a few of us were quietly treading water alongside. By this time, I found

After a serious car crash that resulted in a plate in his forehead, MGM built up Van Johnson's image as the "all-American boy" by co-starring him in films with June Allyson and Esther Williams, among others. He also had his fair share of serious roles in films such as "A Guy Named Joe," "Week-End at the Waldorf," "Thirty Seconds Over Tokyo" and "Battleground." Johnson appeared in more than 80 films.

Van Johnson and Esther Williams in "Easy To Wed," 1946.

myself practically exhausted from the two-hour waterlogged workout. We were all either swimming, floating, treading water or dog paddling, being careful not to make waves or splash, so as not to detract from the dialogue taking place only a few feet away.

There were the usual breaks from time to time, and no more than two shots were completed before lunch. Lunch time was always a wonderful time of complete relaxation for a small group of us who brought our lunches and sat near the long table filled with urns of coffee where we filled our cups during the leisurely luncheon. To all of us, this was far more enjoyable and cheaper than sitting in the studio dining room.

Although her stand-in had been working for more than an hour preparing for the next shot, it was nearly two hours following the lunch break before Esther returned to do her first dive. Because this was my first time working with her, it gave me an opportunity to witness something that turned out to be a surprise.

Like most moviegoers, I thought the star swimmer did all of her own diving. I was amazed to see that when the director called, "Roll 'em!" Esther went up the ladder and out onto the diving board, stood for a moment, then lean forward and bounced. What followed, however, was not what I expected. Instead of seeing her rise up and curve into an arch, then descend into the water below, I heard the director's voice call, "Cut!" With that, Esther turned around, descended the ladder and walked back to her chair.

Her double, wearing a duplicate swimsuit and hair-do (complete with flowers et al), ascended the ladder, walked out on the diving board and stood exactly as Esther had. She hesitated until she heard the words "Roll 'em" then leaning forward, bent her knees and bounced just as Esther had done only moments before. This time, though, there was more than a bounce. She rose into the air, arched into a beautiful dive, and seconds later disappeared into the quiet water not far from where I was seated on the deck. I heard "Cut!" as the double swam to the edge of the pool and climbed out. There was a brief huddle between director, cameraman, and gaffer (senior electrician). When they'd finished, Esther left her chair again, walked to the edge of the pool and slipped into the water. She held the ledge of the pool as the make-up man and hairdresser gave her face and hair a final check, then let go and swam quietly out beneath the diving board, making as little turbulence in the water as possible.

I watched her tread water in the exact spot where her double had disappeared a short time before, careful not to move out of camera range until, given a signal from the director, she took a deep breath, held her nose and disappeared beneath the surface. Moments later, camera rolling and water ablaze with lights, the quiet surface of the water broke and there in all her glory was the smiling face of none other than Miss Esther Williams, not a hair out of place or a single flower askew in her perfect coronet.

Now for me the spell was broken. Though I was surprised and fascinated, I was also disappointed to see for the very first time exactly how it was done.

One of the dramatic films Norman appeared in while not dancing, "Hold High the Torch," starred Lassie. Norman is on the far right.

CHAPTER FIFTEEN

Lassie ... What a Dog!

Lassie, the wonderful canine most folks think of as a girl dog was, if the truth be told, not a she but a he. Like most others, I'd personally never given it a thought one way or the other until one day while working on a film with her (him). The script called for Lassie to get soaking wet. The scene was shot and it was over and done with. It was late in the day and they needed one more shot before calling it quits, otherwise it meant overtime. Ordinarily this would have caused no problem, but for whatever reason on this particular day it wasn't feasible.

Since the crew knew what was coming with the wet dog scene, they had, unbeknownst to me, used another Lassie for the scene. The scene coming up actually took place before Lassie got soaked and they'd slipped in the stand-in. So Lassie is now completely dry, because the dog was never wet in the first place.

Oblivious to all of this, I somehow became interested in just what was going on between Lassie and a couple of guys from the wardrobe Department. Rod Weatherwax, Lassie's owner-trainer, was bending down, patting and speaking to the dog while the guys from wardrobe were attempting to fit her (him) with some sort of custom-created jockstrap covered with fur!

One of the crew told me this type of thing wasn't usually necessary, but that I should watch the next scene to see why they were going to the trouble this time. In the next shot Lassie had to sit up and bark as the camera was doing a close frontal shot. I got it now. They didn't want to shock the public by revealing that the star was really a male!

There was also another time when I earned bread-and-butter in a no-dance film with Lassie. The story line and entire atmosphere proved to be about as unrelated to my usual work as one could possibly imagine. This was a time of war in our country and we were engaged in a filmed war that, when completed, cut, and edited, was just as convincing to a theatre audience. I'd accepted a dual role for a film called *Hold High the Torch*, directed by Richard Thorpe and starring Tom Drake with Lassie. In one role, I briefly appeared as a radio operator in scenes with both Tom and Lassie. In the other instance, I was cast as a regular Army G.I. fighting the battle of Attu.

Had you walked on to Stage 29 during the weeks we were shooting, you would've sworn you'd been magically transported to Attu. The surroundings where we were working were so real they included cliffs and rocky terrain covered with ice and fog. The only light in the scene was from an on-going burst of shells all around. During one sequence when the camera was rolling, it seemed all Hell broke loose as I stepped on one of the planted land mines, which triggered at least half-dozen others in the immediate vicinity. Amidst fire, smoke, shrieks and shots from others around, I staggered for

Norman, second from right, in his second role as radio operator in "Hold High the Torch."

a moment, lost my grip on the rock, slid on slippery ice and fell backward to the ground, at the same time losing my rifle and bayonet. All I could think was, *I hope all this comes out all right so we won't have to shoot it over again. If it's good, then Mr. Thorpe will surely help get my contract changed from dancing to acting.* All of this went through my mind until I heard Thorpe call: "Cut!" He immediately made his way to where I lay on my back, eyes still closed, and asked in all seriousness, "Norman... are you all right?"

Needless to say, not only was I all right, I was feeling great! A number of the crew even applauded. One Grip walked over to me to say he thought it was the greatest dying scene he'd ever witnessed on film. Coming from this particular guy, I needed nothing more. His words of approval more than compensated for the bruises I wore for the next few weeks.

To cap it all off, Lassie, during all of this, had crawled back to my side even before Thorpe had called 'Cut', making her way over the landmine after the explosion, whining and licking me on the face before anyone had checked me out. Whatta dog! From that day, I loved Lassie even more ... regardless of gender.

CHAPTER SIXTEEN

Katharine Hepburn ... And Other MGM Ladies

There are times in all our lives when we discover interesting things outside our usual sphere of knowledge. Though in my particular case I was contracted to dance, it was not long before I discovered other personalities besides the stars who remained an everyday part of my life during the years I spent at MGM.

There is one personality in particular I shall never forget. At one time in the history of films, she had been a star. All movie fans knew her name during the '20s and '30s, particularly at the time, she became leading lady to the one and only Al Jolson in *The Jazz Singer* as well as appearing as Esther in *Ben Hur*. Her name? May McAvoy.

Often while working together, whether doing small bits on the lot or sometimes on location, we talked about lots of things during the lulls in filming. May was working under extremely rare circumstances, having been given a lifetime contract by MGM. I often wondered how she felt about being able to earn movie star money for doing little more than working as an extra. She was one of the early movie stars who didn't survive the transition from silent films to talkies. Though she never discussed it, when others talked about the past, I could clearly see the hurt in her eyes. To me she was a constant reminder of the fragile world of fame that can be here today and gone tomorrow.

Like May, there was another unsung heroine who graced the MGM lot daily. Few people knew Gertrude Fogler, a white-haired little woman who was long past middle age with twinkling eyes and a low, mellow speaking voice which belied her obvious age. For many years she was the voice and diction coach on the MGM lot, which is also why so few people came in contact with her. Her workshop bungalow was tucked away in a remote area not far from men's wardrobe and the property department, and was rarely visited by anyone other than stars or, as in my own case, those few individuals being groomed for a chance at stardom.

Rich, talented, and already famous Katharine Hepburn, whom I'd admired along with Garbo since my high school days in Idaho, was one of Gertrude's regulars. I'd first seen Ms. Hepburn about a year before, when I started at the studio. She was coming out of an office as I was going in. Because my

May McAvoy appeared in such films as "Ben Hur," top left and "The Jazz Singer," top right, during the 1920s.

reason for being there was important and my mind was otherwise occupied, I didn't give seeing her a second thought. I saw movie stars every day, and I guess I'd just become used to it.

Through the first year of my contract there were no lessons with Gertrude Fogler for me. It was only after having worked with director Richard Thorpe a number of times that he spoke to me one day regarding the possibility of switching my contract from dancing to acting. "Norman," he told me, "I have a strong feeling you'd be a fine actor if given the chance. I'd like to talk to Arthur Freed about it." Freed was one of the two most powerful producers on the MGM lot! I thanked Thorpe profusely and he'd be in touch one way or the other.

A few days later I was at home when the call came asking if I'd be free to see Mr. Freed at 2 o'clock that afternoon. "Don't worry about being home later in the day," the voice from the casting office told me, "because I've already checked and there's no call for you tomorrow." I was nearly bowled over by the excitement I was feeling.

That afternoon, just as I was entering Mr. Freed's office, Katharine Hepburn and I nearly bumped one another at the door. The door closed behind me and I stopped dead in my tracks. Across the huge office at least fifty feet ahead, stood a man with his back to me. He was looking out a huge window that overlooked a portion of the studio lot. It was quiet and neither of us moved or spoke. An eternity passed before I was able to cough to announce my presence. It was answered with a single word "Yes?"

There was another awkward silence, maybe fifteen seconds, before I could find my voice. "Mr. Freed, my name is Norman Borine." Thank God, I'd been afraid I'd never be able to put together a coherent sentence! "Mr. Thorpe spoke to me the other day about …"

Katharine Hepburn was a fellow student in Gertrude Fogler's voice and diction classes.

Photo by Clarence Bull

Before I completed my sentence, he turned in my direction, speaking as he walked directly to the largest desk I had ever seen in my life. He seated himself, at the same time directing me to a chair nearby. Before I could thank him, he opened one of the drawers and flipped through a small sheath of papers. "Yes, I know." His voice sounded neither interested nor disinterested. "Mr. Thorpe briefly discussed the subject yesterday. Since I know nothing of your background, I can judge your possibilities only from your looks and your voice as you spoke to me just now." He glanced again at the papers in his hand. Whether or not one of them related to me in any way, I had no idea. "I'll have my secretary call Miss Fogler to begin working with you as soon as she has an opening. You'll hear from her or casting before the end of the week. I'll let Mr. Thorpe know I've spoken with you."

He pushed a button on the desk, nodded politely and wished me a good afternoon. The huge double doors opened as though at his command, and his secretary, pen and pad in hand, walked in. I half walked, half floated out of his office.

The timing was perfect. There was nothing coming up for me for the balance of the week. The day following my odd interview found me seated in the small and comfortable waiting room in Miss Fogler's bungalow. Relaxed, I let my thoughts wander as I waited. At the point when my thoughts were forming a silent thank you to the universe for bringing me to this point in my life, the door to the next room opened and to my astonishment the woman coming toward me was none other than Katharine Hepburn!

Now, years later, I can still hear Miss Fogler saying politely, "Miss Hepburn, this is my newest student. We haven't even met yet." She paused, looked directly into my eyes and spoke my name in such a warm and friendly manner that I immediately felt we'd known one another for a long time. Miss Hepburn, with a smile of acknowledgment, assured me I was in excellent hands. She nodded to us both and left the bungalow.

This began a long series of brief but increasingly meaningful meetings connecting the three of us. Regardless of our varied schedules of rehearsing, shooting, or recording, Hepburn and I seemed to be scheduled with Miss Fogler in back to back appointments. She was cool at first, but warmed as time went on. Eventually each of us was comfortable enough to start using first names when speaking to each other.

When we last met, years after I left the studio, it was at a stop sign on the Sunset Strip. We were side by side in our cars waiting for the light to change, when at the same moment we glanced over and recognized each other. Kate leaned toward me, rolled down the window of her station wagon and called out "Helllloooooo! So nice to see a face that reminds me of other days!" The light changed, and as her window went up she called, "G'bye now ... and remember to follow your dreams!" Her voice was as clear and infectious as her smile. She turned left, disappearing onto the side street toward home as I continued along Sunset Boulevard, smiling as I recalled days gone by.

Cyd Charisse and I had been working with Bronislava Nijinska, sister of the great Nijinsky, just prior to arriving at MGM, which we did within only a few months of one another. Soon we became partners in the fabulous musical extravaganza, "Ziegfeld Follies."

Norman, pictured below, is costumed as a warrior for "On an Island with You," which co-starred Cyd.

To Norman —
Best wishes for
your Hollywood
Palm Springs
project! —
Sincerely,
Cyd Charisse

CHAPTER SEVENTEEN

Cyd Charisse and the Mad Doctor

A few years after Cyd Charisse and I appeared in, then disappeared from, the fantastic "Limehouse Blues" number in *Ziegfeld Follies*, we found ourselves once more working together. This time, however, not as partners. In the new film, she appeared as co-star with Ricardo Montalban. A group of contract dancers appeared with them in a jungle routine in one scene for the film.

Rehearsals for this exotic number lasted more than three weeks. Then, similar to the way I appeared with Betty Hutton prior to my MGM contract (feathers and all), we all began the difficult part — shooting. The contract dancers were made up as colorful savages carrying elaborate long spears. The scene took place atop the third level of a step pyramid. Each level was approximately three feet higher than the other.

For someone like me who's not exactly comfortable with heights, I found it extremely difficult to quiet my mind while dancing atop these elevations. Even the reminder that I was being paid to do this didn't sufficiently calm my nerves, particularly when the choreography required us to perform triple pirouettes repeatedly from the highest level.

Regardless of my reaction to the technical combinations and height requirements, rehearsals finished and shooting began. For more than a week all went well. Because of the strenuous routine, almost as grueling as my first movie, *Ali Baba and the Forty Thieves,* I suspended my evening ballet classes. I decided I should just take it easy in the evenings.

Each day the director and choreographer found it necessary to do things over, sometimes repeating a shot as many as five or six times. Sometimes it was even more, which made the days seem longer and longer.

The entire daily routine was not exactly easy. Up at 5 a.m., then breakfast in time to catch the red car at 5:45, transfer to a bus in Beverly Hills and arrive at Venice and Overland at 6:45. This gave me just time to get to the gate promptly at 7 a.m. There was no clock to punch, instead we checked in with the guard at the gate. Sometimes I managed to squeeze in time for a cup of coffee in the commissary before hurrying along the studio streets past offices, and stars' dressing rooms on my way downstairs to makeup where the famous Westmores would turn all of our faces into exactly what the script called for. Since we were wearing masks that matched our brief, colorfully beaded and feathered costumes, makeup didn't take much time. In my case, since I spent so much time at the beach getting sun, there was little I needed in the makeup department, aside from an all-over sponge-job with just the correct shade of tan to satisfy the cameraman.

We were in our second week of shooting and things were going well, even the number of necessary re-takes. On what had been planned as our next to last day, we were dancing atop the highest pinnacle of the pyramid ramp, whirling, twirling, and leaping through the air like true savages. Then just as we'd rehearsed, Cyd pirouetted and leaped from the top of the ramp to the one below. She was spinning and turning along the ramp with us in pursuit ... until it happened! This time as she leaped into the air, soaring like a bird in flight, her long beautifully shaped legs extended before her toward the earth; the sounds of the heavily orchestrated music covered her first scream as she suddenly crumpled to the ground. Before the director could call 'Cut,' she was screaming and writhing in pain.

The music stopped and the lights went up. There was complete chaos on the huge sound stage. I recall being hopelessly transfixed, looking down at Cyd from the upper level.

149

Norman poses for a "sneak" photo outside the soundstage while working with Cyd Charisse in "On an Island With You." (No cameras were allowed on the MGM lot unless they were sanctioned by the publicity department.)

Mere seconds separated the time between her leap and mine, since I was to follow behind her. I heard someone calling the hospital emergency team. People began moving faster now, some rushing through the door to seek outside assistance, others pushing back the giant sliding door, making room to allow light and fresh air.

Nothing anyone did seemed to lessen the pain of the still crying and screaming victim as she lay on the floor. Guards and others bent over her in an attempt to calm her while they waited for medical help, which came in the form of the studio doctor who was really a nurse.

Quickly bending down on one knee she attempted to move Cyd, which only brought forth renewed shrieks of agony. Obviously frustrated and annoyed, the so-called doctor ordered her four male attendants to place Cyd on a canvas stretcher. As carefully as possible, amidst more shrieks from the victim. I still have difficulty believing what happened next. I distinctly recall hearing the white-clothed "mad doctor" shout an order for the attendants to all line up along one side of the canvas and "Lift!"

For a long second the four turned to her as did everyone in the vicinity, not believing their ears. In an even louder and more demanding voice came a repeat command: "I said lift! And do it now!" Mechanically the soldier-like attendants took places along one side of the stretcher, bent down, lifted ... and the obvious happened! Cyd rolled screaming off the stretcher onto the bare cement floor. What followed was a nightmare of angry voices shouting as the "mad doctor" continued to shout orders. Meanwhile, Cyd lay almost forgotten, writhing in pain.

Someone finally took command and got the four attendants placed at the four corners of the stretcher so they could lift together and carry poor Cyd across the studio street to the MGM hospital. Soon after, she was transferred to a real hospital.

CHAPTER EIGHTEEN

Marlene Dietrich

Years ago, Greta Garbo, a giant among all motion picture giants, chose not to risk diminishing her image in the eyes of the fickle and judgmental public by retiring while at the peak of her game. Books and articles make serious attempts to enlighten curious minds as to the success or failure of this greatest of all female movie stars. Katharine Hepburn, undoubtedly closest to Garbo in a sort of rivalry, made an opposite decision and bravely faced the public as she aged. Foremost among those who have attempted to have their cake and eat it too. Miss Hepburn triumphed in her endeavor.

I'd had one brief glimpse of Dietrich on the day I entered the fabled land of MGM to sign my unbelievable contract. So, I was absolutely delighted one afternoon when I answered my telephone and heard these words, "Norman, please report to Paramount tomorrow morning at nine, with rehearsal clothes for a dance number with Marlene Dietrich. The picture is *Golden Earrings*, and the choreographer will be Billy Daniels. You'll be working there for about three weeks. Following that, we expect to have something for you here, something I know you'll like a lot." That was it, and for the balance of the day, I floated among the clouds.

I leaped out of bed the next morning. I recall waking before the alarm went off in order to shave, shower, have a good breakfast and arrive at the studio five minutes early.

For nearly a week, during which Marlene was engaged in shooting dialogue scenes, six guys and six girls rehearsed simple movements to the theme song for the film *Golden Earrings*. A dance-in for Marlene was in place and we were hardly more than dramatic body-expressions creating a sort of background for the star as she sang seductively to the camera.

To me, personally, just watching Marlene each day from the moment she entered the rehearsal hall until she disappeared at the end of a day, was like watching the sun make its way through a sometimes-cloudy sky. There were no doubts that this number would be a complete success, despite its technical simplicity. By this time, I'd become used to seeing stars, but Dietrich was decidedly different. I continued to stare at her every move, even when she simply walked through the routine with us. I was mesmerized and seduced all over again, just like when I was a teenager.

I can still hear her voice, see her face, and feel her hand as I moved her into a slow turn, matching movement to the words of the song she was singing. (If it weren't for the reality of the keys on my typewriter, I might easily be convinced it was all happening again as I replay the memory ever so slowly in my mind.)

It truly didn't matter to me what part of our simple dance in *Golden Earrings* actually ended up on film. The experience was enough for me this time.

A decidedly un-glamorous Marlene Dietrich in "Golden Earrings."

A few days after we began shooting the routine, Marlene seemed to be in a bad mood. When the assistant told us to take a break, I wasted no time approaching her and asking if I might have a photo when we finished shooting. Her voice sounded beautiful as was her smile when she looked me right in the eyes, and said simply, "Well, they just called a break, so why don't we walk over to my bungalow and get one for you now?" Though it was a question, it was at the same time a statement. My smile was my answer.

Like Judy along the Yellow Brick Road, Marlene and I followed the soft red carpet (something I had never seen before, or since), which the studio had laid out along the ground all the way from the sound stage to her private bungalow. I can still feel the softness of that thick carpet, and I recall her soft husky voice inviting me to sit and relax while she looked for the photo. My eyes wandered, taking inventory of the room while I waited for her. I could hear her speaking to someone. Then, as though following a script, she returned with three 8 x 10 glossy photos and asked me to "just pick one, and would you like me to autograph it for you?" My answer was obvious.

She was in the act of signing the photo I'd chosen when her personal maid appeared, carrying a silver tray laden with a beautiful pot of steaming hot tea, two matching cups, and a small tray of cookies. The maid asked if I would, "care for sugar, cream, lemon … and how much." I felt like a king!

Fifteen minutes later Marlene and I were retracing our steps along the red carpet as I mentally thanked the cosmos for this once in a lifetime experience.

Marlene Dietrich poses in her usual glamorous state.

James Dean sometimes joined Norman and his volleyball buddies on the beach.

CHAPTER NINETEEN

James Dean

James Dean, from the day he arrived on the Hollywood scene, was an enigma . My own experiences with him were limited, but most assuredly not forgotten. I met him before fame had saddled him with insecurities and self-imposed tortures which followed him to the very day of his death. A death, which like Marilyn Monroe, Montgomery Clift, Bruce and Brandon Lee, and others, was far too soon.

No one can say I hung out with Jimmy during my last year at MGM, because he was important and a star. Our first encounter was during the time he was enrolled as a student at Santa Monica City College studying pre-law and physical education. He showed up at Will Rogers State Beach one Saturday where our volleyball group met on a regular basis.

I never bothered to ask Jimmy who brought him or how he came to join us, probably because I sensed he'd simply shrug his shoulders and ask what difference it made. For a time we simply said "Hi" to each other, nothing more. I was 14 years older than he, we discovered later, but this was of little consequence. Neither of us, at the time, seemed to be too attracted to each other. One Saturday, though, as we prepared to leave the beach and head across the Highway to Doc Law's, out of the blue Jimmy yelled at me, "I'll race you to the water!" and off he went.

Had I stopped to think I would've wondered what brought this on, but I didn't. Instead, off I ran across the sand not ten steps behind him, diving along with him under a huge wave that threw us beneath its surface. When we emerged only seconds apart, we were laughing like a couple of school kids. Both of us felt like a million dollars as we joined the rest of the group who merely shook their heads without verbalizing what was running through their minds. Perhaps, at least subconsciously, it was running through ours as well.

For a long moment Jimmy forgot where he'd dropped his glasses and seemed to almost panic before one of the guys spied them at the foot of the post holding the net. They were undamaged except for having a little sand on them, much to Jimmy's relief. Those thick-lensed, horn-rimmed glasses were obviously a definite part of his personal identity, and his most worrisome possession. Without them, he could easily become totally frustrated, and momentarily fall apart.

As we crossed the Pacific Coast Highway, someone made a remark about people who do crazy things for no reason. Head lowered in typical Dean manner, Jimmy half-turned to me and said somewhat caustically, "Why does there always have to be a reason? Can't a guy do something just because he wants to?" I glanced back at him with an attempt to copy his facial expression … half in wonderment, half in jest. And that was how we got together. We just felt like it.

James Dean

Doc Law's was no fancy place by anyone's definition. It was just an old, stained, wooden building where all of us felt comfortable. We enjoyed ourselves at wooden tables on one side of the room, or hung our legs over old bar stools on the opposite side. Food, though seldom more than a fat juicy hamburger with fries, was their specialty, and the beer was good and cold. This was one of those places where brews were served up in giant frosted mugs. Nearly every Saturday it was the same, we'd end our day there, relaxing, sometimes until late evening, before heading back home. We were a diverse group, though most of us were in the same business.

The following Saturday Jimmy didn't show up. I wondered where he was, but didn't think much about it. A week later I heard a familiar voice as I headed down the cement steps onto the sand. "I'll race ya to the water, and the last one in is a rotten egg." I looked through the bodies mingling around the net before I spied him, hardly recognizing him minus the glasses. They'd become the primary thing I identified him by, that along with his slouch and general melancholy face.

"Later," was my reply. "Gimme a rain-check, 'til after the second game. I'm pooped right now." Jimmy immediately looked disappointed, and headed for the water alone … walking, not running. This was the first time I sensed that the word "alone" best described Jimmy.

At some point that summer, I recall Jimmy mentioning moving in with another student at Santa Monica City College. Though I never had the feeling he didn't get along with his father, I had a definite awareness he was not comfortable living with him. He seldom spoke of him or of his recent shift to an apartment with a roommate. Looking back, this may have been one of our strong attractions to one another.

There were evenings after Doc Law's, aside from our regular Saturday clambakes, when we would decide to just toss everything into the car and drive up to Malibu or Dana Point. Malibu was fine for

For Norman, the
word "alone"
best described
his friend,
James Dean.

just strolling along the beach or sitting down near the water and sharing ideas. A few times, though, when we both had that undeniable and urgent gnawing sensation and wanted to do something about it, we'd head for The Point. Weather often had something to do with it. One time, I clearly remember, it was the moon. We could hardly wait to get down the trail from the top of the cliff, doff our shorts and sandals, and begin chasing each other, before falling over one another in a heap.

These few times are among the most carefree expressions I've experienced in my life … times when all thoughts of anything except pure joy were left a thousand miles behind. In those rare and treasured moments, it was as if we were in another world. There was nothing we didn't do with each other, to each other, for each other. It was as if nothing could separate us mentally, emotionally or physically as we walked, ran, wrestled and laughed. It was complete and utter abandonment until at last, exhausted, we totally collapsed, begging each other to stop.

Sleep sometimes claimed us before we realized it. Once the sleep was so deep it took the quiet lapping of waves across our bodies to finally awakened us. It was then that we became like two little kids, laughing (in Jimmy's case, giggling) at ourselves and diving again into the icy-cold water. Minutes later, arms draped across one another's shoulders, we'd slowly head back along the sand in search of shorts and sandals as we headed up the trail to the car.

On the evening of September 20, 1955, a mutual friend phoned me. With his very first words, I sensed death. "Did you hear about Jimmy?" was all he needed to ask. To this day, I can't think of Jimmy without memories of Dana Point. Each time, I'm compelled to take a mental trip and head back down that trail to the beach and walk naked along the sand until I fall exhausted.

James Dean

Judy Garland

CHAPTER TWENTY

Judy — An Untold Story

Annie Get Your Gun promised to be a new high in the roller coaster career of Judy Garland. Bob Alton, still the number one choreographer in the movie industry, was exuberant as he began putting us through experimental dance combinations for the big Indian number. Judy, still involved in shooting dialogue on another stage, popped into the rehearsal hall occasionally, usually to confer with Kay Thompson, her vocal coach, and Roger Edens, pianist. She would also check out how we were getting along with the number.

Since we were by no means finished with the choreography of the Big Pow Wow, we were still featherless. However, we'd been shown sketches of the costumes wardrobe had dreamed up, and they were colorful, dramatic, and exciting. I began to question just exactly what it was about me that made me so perfect for scenes requiring feathered costumes. This would be the fourth time I'd appeared in films calling for me to be clothed in feathers: *Incendiary Blonde*, with Betty Hutton, *Ziegfeld Follies*, with Cyd Charisse, *On an Island with You*, again with Cyd, and now *Annie Get Your Gun*, with Judy.

Judy's number was "I'm an Indian, Too." Having completed her dialogue sequences, she joined us in Rehearsal Hall A, where we sang and danced together. It created a wonderful atmosphere of togetherness as we now unhurriedly worked day after day on this project. Toward the end of rehearsals, J. Carroll Naish, who appeared as the Chief, joined us for approximately a week to stage his scenes. His part had little to do with the actual dance, and related only to dialogue with Judy when we Indians surrounded them.

During lunch break, most of us guys (Indians, now), wearing as little as possible, would lie around outside the hall and gab and eat our lunches. We all enjoyed this and it helped to shorten our time in makeup. Mostly we just had to have enough makeup to cover the shine.

Since we had no access to a refrigerator, we kept lunches in our lockers downstairs in the dressing rooms. Each noontime we'd flip a coin to see who would make a mad dash to the liquor store across the street from the studio to get ice-cold sodas. This added a bit of luxury and to our simple meals.

It was Friday afternoon, and we'd had a long day that began at 7 a.m. The first shot had been lined up Thursday afternoon, including camera moves, lighting, and all other technicalities except those, which could be done only prior to the director's call for action. The entire morning went well and the shot received approval from director Arthur Freed after only the second take. Judy and Naish were then excused for lunch while the rest of us, including part of the crew, remained long enough to do partial set-up for the next shot.

Everyone returned from lunch on schedule, thinking this final shot would be simple as far as camera moves and lighting were concerned. By three o'clock it was "ready on the set." As expected, the shot was complete and double-checked by the assistant before he called out, "Wrap-em up!" We were all prepared to celebrate the conclusion of this last great number.

Walking past the camera while removing my elaborate headdress, I couldn't help but notice the sudden formation of a group of technicians and executives only a few feet away, obviously involved in some sort of serious discussion. Seconds later, the whistle sounded and the assistant picked up the microphone, "Okay everyone, listen up!" He hesitated for a moment, turned toward Freed who whispered something to him, then continued, "I know tomorrow is Saturday, so everyone listen closely. Come in the morning at the usual time for one re-take. We expect to finish before noon. That's it."

There was confusion everywhere, obviously due to the forced change of plans for the weekend. We grouped together here and there, discussing what the cause of this sudden re-call might be. Gradually people began to move away across the huge set and out through the giant door into the late afternoon sun. It felt good for a change, being outside at this time of day. I headed for the gate, wondering what tomorrow would bring. There was somehow a note of sadness following me as I made my way slowly toward the trolley. It continued all the way home, and was still with me the next morning. I had no idea what was about to happen and how everything was going to change.

As usual, I reported to makeup, where one of the team applied an Indian-like transformation to my face, followed by minimum body make-up for my good tan. There was still plenty of time before going to the set, so I walked over to the commissary and sat down with an empty seat on each side of me. In a matter of seconds I felt a hand on my shoulder and heard a familiar voice asking enthusiastically, "May I sit down?" Without waiting for a reply, the owner of the voice sat down in the empty seat on my left.

Pete Lawford, approached from the other side, asking, "If it's not too personal, do you mind if I join you? Its obvious you don't intend to be among the elite at the beach today … so what's up?"

Robert Walker, the voice on my left, was by no means a comedian. However, on this particular morning he was in top form, wearing a grin that stretched from one ear to the other. Both of the guys were headed to wardrobe, and informed me they were only on the lot for fittings. They were each working on different pictures, and both expected to have their respective work over and done with long before noon. As he headed for the door, Pete again urged me to "get it over with and get yourself down to the beach."

Robert's parting message was thoughtful and simple: "Give Judy my love and tell her I hope everything will be all right."

Promptly at nine o'clock, I watched Judy greet the director before entering her portable dressing room. The crew had been at work since 7 a.m., and at 9:30 Judy stepped out of her door and onto the set where everyone was ready. I sensed everyone wanted to do it and get it over so we could go home, therefore I was totally surprised to see that Judy wasn't in makeup. That was especially odd, since I'd seen someone carrying her costume into the dressing room. In one corner of the stage, a circus-type tent had been set up for us (Indians) as a dressing room, which saved time going back and forth to wardrobe. Each of us needed help to get into our costumes, particularly the feather headdresses.

The setting for our retake was a huge rock where Judy and the chief (J. Carroll Naish) sat beside each other with rigid, straight postures, looking directly out at us Warriors with serious looks on their faces. We, in turn, formed a huge semi-circle in front of them. The camera was behind, shooting over our shoulders. All at once, Freed called out, "Quiet on the set. This is a rehearsal."

As Judy Garland
got older, the studio
tried to make her fit
their image of what a
leading lady should
look like by giving her
"sexier" wardrobe,
hair and makeup.

Judy, still looking straight ahead with a deadpan expression, directed a five word question to the chief: "Am I an Indian yit?" And in like-manner, the chief answers in a deep drawl: "Naaawt yit!"

That was the entire scene. Nothing more. The rehearsal went well and Freed spoke to members of the crew, then asked Judy to get made-up. I could easily see her make-up man, wardrobe lady, and hairdresser all standing by, waiting for her. In less than an hour, we Warriors were dressed, ready to go, and I noticed the make-up man leaving Judy's dressing room just as the others went in. Thirty minutes later, Judy came out and walked across the set. She casually took her place beside the chief and they greeted one another and spoke briefly while waiting for Freed to call out his orders.

Perhaps, had all of us known what was running through Judy's mind at this particular time, what was about to happen might have been avoided. But, it would probably have happened … sooner or later. The back of the proverbial camel was destined to break, and I can only tell it the way it happened.

All was ready. Everything was in place. When Freed called out, "Roll 'em!" I'm certain he, too, felt this would be quick and all of us would be headed home. Judy, staring off into space, looked straight into our faces, and apparently some individual had a funny look on his face which triggered something Judy couldn't control. As she solemnly asked the chief, "Am I an Indian yit?" she broke into sudden, uncontrollable laughter.

Fred immediately called, "Cut!" Trying to ignore it, he followed up with, "Quiet, everyone. Let's try it again." This reaction was not particularly unusual for a star, and she seemed to recover as Freed again called, "Roll 'em!" This time, all went well during the delivery of her line, but when the chief answered in his usual deep and serious voice. Judy again erupted with laughter that she couldn't seem to stop.

Judy, following a succesful performance at the Greek Theatre in Hollywood, signed this special photo for Norman.

I wondered if it was something Judy was thinking, or if one of our Indian brothers was truly encouraging the situation through some facial expression. Again Freed made an attempt to ignore the problem and for the third time we witnessed Judy cracking-up. Controlling himself perfectly, Freed made one last try. During this time, none of us noticed Bob Alton move quietly to one side, away from the camera, to a place where he could observe us, unobstructed. Following the usual orders from Freed, Judy started laughing with the very first word out of her mouth. The director was now disturbed, and it showed. As we heard the word "Cut," Bob Alton grabbed a microphone and ordered, "Every single dancer, go to the dressing room! Now!"

In the dressing room tent, Alton started raging at us. Even those he'd brought from New York later said they'd never seen him in such a fury. He held nothing back as he shouted at us, "I have never in my entire life been so angry or so ashamed! Ashamed of what I just saw out there! How dare you do this to that poor girl. She's already sick and needs all the love and help she can get! You, and you know who you are, have the nerve to make faces and cause her to fall apart!" Bob was trembling, one hand clenched in a fist, the other pointing a finger toward all of us. "Let's get this shot!"

Needless to say, we were speechless. We walked back on to the set. We were quiet and subdued, but already it was too late. Judy had spoken to Freed and the camera crew, asking permission to break for lunch before returning to make the single shot … the one never to become a reality. Though it was early, her request was granted.

Over the loudspeakers, we heard these words: "Two hours, everyone. Back at 1:30, then we'll wrap-it-up and go home." The voice sounded cheerful. No one on that giant stage had the least idea what would or would not happen.

None of our group had brought lunch. We all thought we'd be long gone by this time. Mentally, I was at the beach with my buddies. Since destiny had changed our plans, most of us splurged and dined at the commissary. Judy was nowhere to be seen. The large table where she usually sat was filled with executives, but Freed was not among them. We thought something was definitely not right.

Lunch concluded and everyone returned to the set, ready to do our thing and leave. We had broken at 11:30. It was now already after 1:30 and still we waited. Freed arrived alone at exactly 1:45, walking directly over to the camera crew. They stood quietly together in a closely knit huddle, speaking in undertones and glancing about occasionally, as though expecting someone else to join in what was obviously a serious matter.

We watched and waited. A few moments passed, and the group moved their chairs to form a circle, seating themselves and moving forward. This seemed to increase the intensity of their discussion. Within ten minutes, Freed stood up, left the group and walked to the telephone. He spoke briefly, and then returned to his director's chair.

From where I was sitting, I could see the clock, the hands now pointed to 3 o'clock. At that precise moment there was an ominous click from the mike, followed by the assistant's voice. Hesitatingly, he spoke words we were truly unprepared to hear, "Mr. Freed has asked me to inform you that everyone is dismissed. There is no call-back." Again, hesitation, followed by a final statement: "Thanks to all of you for being here today. There is nothing more I can tell you at this time."

The atmosphere on set was like a morgue. Everywhere people spoke in whispers. Nowhere did there seem to be the slightest variation to this tomb-like atmosphere, and I mechanically joined the other Indians as we moved slowly away from it all toward wardrobe. Today, I cannot recall passing through the great iron gates, or as was my custom, nodding to that roaring Leo overhead.

Monday at home, I waited all day, expecting the call that did not come. Newspapers everywhere blared the information I was yet to learn, "Judy Garland Dismissed From MGM." It was tragic and simple. Her lack of control on Saturday was, as we had begun to suspect, the straw that broke the camel's back. We all believed Judy would never again pass beneath the MGM arch she'd figuratively helped to build.

How strange that I am now unable to clearly recall any of the other assignments, other films, other stars with whom I continued to work during the remaining months of my contract before I, too, passed for the last time beneath the arch in 1950. I went on to a summer season of dancing at the outdoor Greek Theatre in Hollywood. Later I would watch Judy perform on that very stage, and afterward visit with her in her dressing room, not knowing I would never see her in person again.

Judy Garland was more than a singer, an actress or a star, she was truly an ideal. She was filled with fantasies, with dreams, with hopes and used them to entertain millions of people around the globe. To all who saw her on the screen, on television or in reality, she gave everything she had to take her audiences into the make-believe world of entertainment.

I can still hear her saying to Auntie Em, "There's no place like home … there's no place … like home."

The author, second from right, showing off his dark, hair color along with star June Vincent in the movie "The Climax."

CHAPTER TWENTY-ONE

The Silver Screen vs Theatre

Sometimes now, allowing thoughts to slip back through the years to those wonderful, glamorous and truly magical experiences I feel like they didn't even exist ... that it was all a childhood dream that began when I spotted the mysterious looking face of Anna May Wong on the cover of *Hollywood* magazine. Can it really be true that I spent seven years in the "magic kingdom" of MGM amidst 57 top stars of the silver screen? Yes, it was the golden age of movie musicals, and on certain days I realize I did so much ... so many different things with so many wonderful individuals ...

Sometimes I'm bothered when I ask myself what I really have to show for it. If, as I've tried to convince myself, I were dancing in a Broadway show today I could grab you by the hand and ask you to, "Come, watch me dance tonight in this great show." Then perhaps you'd come, sit and watch. Maybe you'd laugh. Maybe you'd cry. Or maybe you'd just enjoy the performance. Afterward, when

Leslie Caron starred with Gene Kelly in "An American in Paris," one of the movies using the MGM contract dancers.

for
Norman —
Leslie Caron.
1945

I'd removed my makeup and costume we'd go out for coffee and talk about it. You'd actually see everything I did and have some idea about how long and hard I must've worked during rehearsals before the show opened.

What happens, though, when I attempt to tell you now about all of the great and wonderful times I had back then … rehearsing sometimes for as many weeks on one number as is spent today to rehearse an entire Broadway production? You watch a rerun on TV, which over the years has been edited and cut a dozen times in order to make room for commercials. You blink as you say to yourself, "Where was our friend, Norman?" It's frustrating as hell to think of what the editor's cutting-shears chose to snip out and let fall to the floor.

Recently, to surprise me, a friend dug out videos of *Meet Me in St. Louis* and *Harvey Girls*. Need I say they were each a case-in-point? We'd spent weeks rehearsing with Judy, as well as my dear old friend, Marjorie Main. Though my friend enjoyed the films and exclaimed, when glimpsing me dancing here and there, "How wonderful it must have felt just to have been there." But I kept trying to explain my feelings about the whole thing and he kept trying to convince me it was okay. I didn't have to try to prove anything to anybody.

"All that's important for you," he kept repeating, "is simply knowing you were there, and being a part of the MGM magic." With that remark, he pushed the button and the film we'd been watching disappeared. I realized once again how things have changed. But yes, perhaps my friend is right. It is okay.

For those who've been a part of the movie industry, there is an awareness that it was no dream. It was very real. Once again I recall the grandiose Stage 30, unlike any in the entire world, and the things that were filmed there. Whether it was being used for an Esther Williams underwater ballet or the finale of some musical masterpiece like *Ziegfield Follies*, there was always that excitement and magical feeling. That sensation when I walked through that door marked NO VISITORS and entered the world of movie make-believe. Even with the passage of time, I still recall how we danced through mist and fog, with stars and show girls floating across the horizon on treadmills. Our togetherness in this fantasy endeavour made each of us know it was all more than just a dream.

The amazing thing about this whole era was that the magic didn't just happen once, it happened over and over again. Like the colossal number to the music of *This Heart Of Mine*, with lyrics by Arthur Freed. The setting for this extravaganza was a huge dining room, domed and as large as an observatory at some planetarium. The magnificent sculptured doors open, and from out of nowhere 30 dancers enter via a moving section of the floor, each posed against a 10-foot leafless frosted tree equipped with invisible rollers. As we pass through the dining room, each of us, one by one, slide our tree effortlessly onto a circular treadmill, which takes us around the eerie winter wonderland where Fred Astaire and Lucille Bremer, centered in the room, dance and sing to the title song.

Fred and all of us guys are in tuxedos; Lucille and the girls are in beautiful formals. Director Minnelli, on the giant boom, is once more in his glory. Just as we had long ago nicknamed Judy "Little Miss One Take" because of her consistent ability to do it right the first time, we also referred to Vincente as the "boom-happy" director.

Another major musical number of similar grandure is the grand finale of *An American In Paris*, which starred Gene Kelly and Leslie Caron. The grand finale is the one of those creations destined to be shown for all time as an example of the golden age of musicals. Indeed, it was so huge it included all of the contract dancers plus many others.

Ten foot tall leafless, frosted trees were equipped with invisible rollers so they could slide effortlessly onto a circular treadmill that went round and round as Fred Astaire and Lucille Bremer danced and sang to "This Heart of Mine" in "Ziegfeld Follies." Norman is pointed out by the arrow.

1325-1

Yes, it was another of the times when I felt frustrated, coming away after viewing the film and saying: "Where was I?" Not only weeks, but often months of creative dancing, followed by weeks of actual filming. Now once again I must convince myself it's okay because I was there. I was a part of it all. Looking back I have nearly as many wonderful memories as there are stars in the sky, and I realize they just don't make 'em like that anymore.

\

The End

Norman Borine

About the Author

To be a contract dancer during the golden age of movie musicals was "akin to being on intimate terms with the gods and goddesses of movieland ... Gene Kelly, Fred Astaire, Cyd Charisse, Esther Williams, Van Johnson, Hedy LaMarr, Lana Turner, Judy Garland ... tripping the light fantastic on Mt. Olympus ... namely, MGM Studios."

The above quote comes from *Nostalgia* magazine, Sept./Oct. 1988, from an article by the late Joan Woodbury, a well-known Hollywood actress who was formerly married to Henry Wilcoxon. The article, in part, goes on to say:

For seven glamorous, terpsichorean years, Norman Borine danced in every great musical released by the roaring lion. Beginning at the low end of the chorus line, Borine went on to become a $1,000 a week in-demand, front and center dancer who never had to leave Hollywood for greener pastures.

"When I was eight, I knew I wanted to be an entertainer" began the tall, blonde, perennial youth. "In college, I read the life of the great Nijinsky and decided I wanted to be a dancer." Hollywood was his destination, where he would learn from some of the greatest names in classical and modern dance, including Ruth St. Denis, Adolph Bolm, Serge Oukrainsky, (former partner of Pavlova), Lester Horton, David Lichine, and Bronislava Nijinsky, sister of the one-and-only Nijinsky. "It seems more than a coincidence," says Norman, "that Nijinsky (in spirit) caused me to become a dancer. Some years later his sister turned out not only to be one of my teachers, but also the individual who sent me on my first movie interview and shortly thereafter signed a letter which enabled me to become a member of the Screen Actors Guild. From that day, I was never without work."

Nijinska's letter to the Guild allowed Norman to begin his exciting career at Universal Studios in *Ali Baba and the Forty Thieves*, starring the glamorous Maria Montez, Jon Hall, and Turhan Bey. He remained there for two more musicals, one starring the young Susanna Foster; the other, Yvonne De Carlo, choreographed by Tilly Losch, brought from London primarily to appear with Gregory Peck and Jennifer Jones in the dramatic epic, *Duel in the Sun*. Following those three films, Norman moved over to Paramount, where he appeared in *Incendiary Blonde* with Betty Hutton.

Almost immediately, the two became close friends and Betty introduced Norman to Raoul Pene Du Bois, well-known New York City costume and set designer, who in turn introduced him to Robert Alton, Broadway choreographer with five hit musicals running concurrently.

He'd recently been lured from stage to movies by MGM, who signed him to the longest and highest salaried contract ever presented to a choreographer. It was he who offered Norman a seven-year contract, having never even seen him dance.

"When Raoul and Betty both recommended him, that was good enough for me," Alton said later. "Furthermore, when I needed someone to partner Cyd Charisse in her first film, *Ziegfeld Follies*, I picked Norman from all of the contract dancers because he and Cyd had worked in classes under Nijinska. Together, they were perfect."

When asked who impressed him more than any star he ever danced with, Norman did not hesitate for a split-second. "Judy Garland", he replied. "My first experience working with her was in *Till the Clouds Roll By* (the story of Jerome Kern). During the entire time, she was carrying Liza. Later, I was in rehearsal on another number the very first time Judy and Vincente walked proudly into the hall to show her off to all of us. It was a great moment, though no one could foretell the future which lay ahead for this special little girl." Years later, Norman and Judy were to work together again at Warner Brothers Studio, in the re-make of an old Janet Gaynor film, *A Star is Born*.

Leaving MGM in 1950, Norman appeared in five Broadway shows during the summer at the famous outdoor Greek Theatre in Hollywood, followed by three months at the Curran Theatre in San Francisco with Gertrude Niesen in the road show of *Gentlemen Prefer Blondes*.

When the season was over, Norman planned to go to New York to find work, but suddenly one morning while preparing for the trip, the phone rang and a beautiful but unfamiliar voice said, "Norman, this is Eleanor Powell. Would it be possible to have breakfast with me tomorrow morning to discuss a new TV show, "Faith of Our Children," I'll be doing for NBC? I saw your work on another channel last week and I'd love to have you as choreographer."

"That experience over the next two years," Norman says, "was the happiest work of my life. Yes, we not only met and had breakfast in a small restaurant at Sunset and Vine, but walked immediately afterward to NBC (at that time, right on the corner) where I signed a contract. From that moment on, Ellie and I became like sister and brother. At the end of two years, the show had won five Emmy Awards and we were ecstatic."

Norman eventually moved to Palm Springs, California. He said, "I've been a dreamer all my life, and it worked. Now, with people like Deepak Chopra and others including my very dear friend, Dr. Ann Martin who helps us better understand ourselves, not only with creativity, but with longevity, I'm realizing more each year that I have a very unique and fascinating story to tell. It's once again: LIGHTS! CAMERA! ACTION! So, if it's going to be, it's up to me, and I know the audience is waiting."

Norman Borine passed away November 27, 2005.

Upon completing his 7-year contract at MGM, Norman became a full-time model at the Hollywood Art Center.

More Glimpses of the
Yellow Brick Road

Judy Garland, for Norman Borine, was forever and always "somewhere over the rainbow."

The "Wizard of Oz" was one of Norman's favorite movies.

More Photos
of Days Gone By

Burt Lancaster worked with Norman at Paramount and they became friends.

Before he became a contract dancer, Norman met Cesar Romero on a studio tour.

"Young, Rich and Pretty," an MGM picutre. Cast included Danielle Darrieux, Jane Powell, and Richard Anderson. Vic Damone and Fernando Lamas made their film debuts in this movie. Norman is pictured second from the right. 1951

Elizabeth Taylor as Cleopatra, a 20th Century Fox film from 1963.

Rudolph

In this scene from "Carnival in Costa Rica," Norman is the first man on the left. The film starred Dick Haymes, Vera Ellen, Cesar Romero and Carrol Naish.

Norman enjoyed dancing with Mitzi Gaynor in more than one film during one of his many loan-outs.

To Norman —
Every good good wish
for your happiness and happiness
Sincerely —
Mitzi Gaynor

Greta Garbo

Greta Garbo was one of Norman's favorite female stars.

Gretta Garbo

In this scene depicting the tormented mind of Dr. Hohnor (Boris Karloff), Marcellina (Susanna Foster) returns to haunt him in "The Climax." Norman is the first visible man on the right.

1944

Another scene from "The Climax," with Suzanna Foster. Norman is pictured third from the left in the top row of men.

F. Franklin

To Norman Borine
Good wishes
Paulette Goddard

Paulette
Goddard

Ethel
Merman

Gretta Garbo strikes a seductive pose.

greta garbo

Richard
Denning

Mae West
was a close
neighbor when
Norman lived
in Hollywood.

Dustin Hoffman

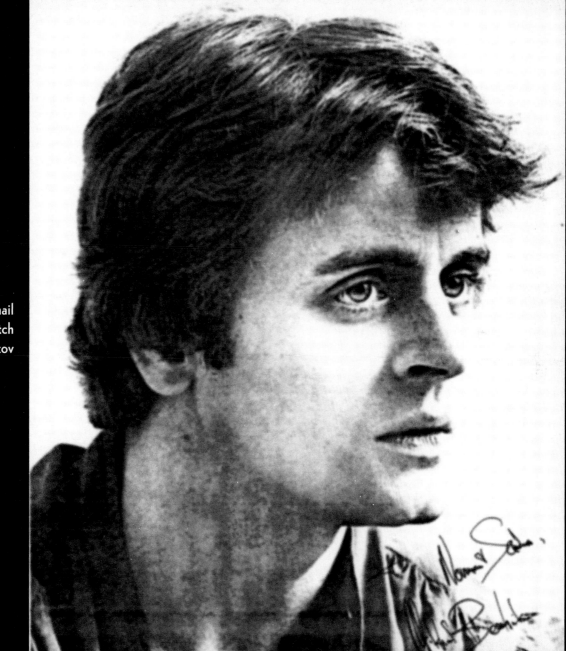

Mikhail
Nikolaevitch
Baryshnikov

Eleanor Powell

ELEANOR POWELL

GIVE SOMEONE A BIBLE
(ON CHRISTMAS DAY)
Words and Music by MILLE BECK and ADELE SLOANE

Price 50c
In U.S.A.

Inspired by Eleanor Powell and her "Faith Of Our Children" Television Show

GRANITE MUSIC COMPANY
1651 Cosmo St., Hollywood 28, Calif.

Eleanor Powell chose Norman as choreographer for her NBC television show, Faith of Our Children, which ran for two years during the '50s and won five Emmy Awards. The two became like brother and sister during this time.

Soon after winning the Emmy Awards for her TV show, Ellie made an extended appearance in a Las Vegas nightclub, photos left.

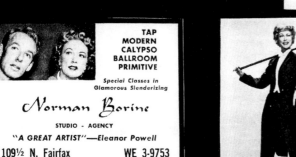

Norman Borine

Norman Borine, Darlene Powell, vocal soloist, Eleanor Powell, star of the show, on set of "Faith of Our Children."

Eleanor Powell holds with one of the five Emmy Awards her show won.

In loving memory of Norman Eddison Boring
November 28, 1917 - November 27, 2005

Norman changed his name to Norman Borine when he entered into the entertainment world with MGM.

Index